Angel Or Devil

LIMITED EDITION

Angel Or Devil

Photography and Art Design by Christopher Saint Booth
Models: Rachel Marie and Ava Aurora
Additional research Denise Mendenhall
Angel Or Devil Art Design ©2016 Christopher Saint Booth
The Possessed ©2009 Spooked Productions.
The Exorcist File ©2014 Spooked Productions
The Haunted Boy ©2010 Spooked Productions
THE EXORCIST DIARY©2015 Spooked Productions
PARANOIA The Strange Case Of Ghosts, Demons and Aliens ©2015 Spooked Productions

This book is distributed as a serious reference study in possession and is not attended in anyway to endorse or exploit any religion or the people portrayed in this book and these true journals.

DEVIL OR ANGEL ©2106 SPOOKED PRODUCTIONS
CHRISTOPHER SAINT BOOTH
Watseka Wonder & Begone Satan © Creative Commons

All Rights Reserved. No part of this publication may be reproduced or transmitted in any form or by any means, electronic or mechanical, including photocopy, recording, or any information storage and retrieval system, without permission in writing from the publisher.

SPOOKED TV PUBLICATIONS 18017 CHATSWORTH STREET #130
GRANADA HILLS, CALIFORNIA, 91344 USA
Email: info@spookedproductions.com
Phone: 310-498-9576

Angel Or Devil

Angel Or Devil

INTRODUCTIONS

WRITTEN BY CHRISTOPHER SAINT BOOTH

from PARANOIA The Strange Case Of Ghosts, Demons and Aliens

and THE EXORCIST DIARY

THE WATSEKA WONDER

by E. W. STEVENS

CHICAGO: RELIGI0-PHILOSOPHICAL PUBLISHING HOUSE. 1878.

BEGONE SATAN

WRITTEN BY REV. CARL VOGL

translated by

REV. CELESTINE KAPSNER, O.S.B.

Spooked TV Publications

ISBN-13:978-0692663646 ISBN-10:0692663649

www.spookedtv.com

Angel Or Devil

INTRODUCTION

THE STRANGE CASE OF THE WATSEKA WONDER

Based on a startling and instructive psychological study. The Watseka Wonder case was also classified as an authentic instance of Angelic visitation. All Spiritualists, and those investigating the subject of Spiritualism will find this case a must read.

The small town of Watseka, Illinois population 5,000 is located about 50 miles south of Chicago and only a few miles from the Indiana border. The sensation that would come to be known as the Watseka Wonder had its beginnings there in July of 1877.

"The Watseka Wonder story, America's first documented possession involving two stories and two families. The first family is the Roff family, they had a daughter, Mary Roff, who died mysteriously when she was 18 years old. Twelve years later in 1877, Lurancy Vennum, a girl who was 14 years old, and lived on the other side of town, who was only two years old when Mary Roff died. She began having her own series of fits and seizures along the same lines that Mary Roff had. At one point Lurancy told the people she was communicating with a spirit that wanted to come into her body, and it was someone who knew someone here

in the town. When the spirit came into her body, and within a few days, Lurancy Vennum, or Lurancy under the power of Mary Roff, had convinced the Roff family that she was indeed their dead daughter."

~John Whitman, Owner of the Watseka Wonder/ Roff House

It was almost winter and the moon was full. Talk about a panic attack driving up to Watseka in the dead of night. On each side of the old highway we were surrounded by miles of barren corn fields. I had visions of being sickled to death. If we were going to run out of gas in the middle of nowhere and be killed, this is exactly where it would go down. Upon arrival, Watseka was a cute little town that had a wonderful old museum and a classic movie theater. It also had a brand new motel where we could rest and hide from the wicked corn monster. We slept for a few hours in the bug infested room. After a quick shower we headed to the first brick house in the Illinois County.

John Whitman owner of the Roff House agreed to open his doors with the promise that we would only tell the Watseka Wonder story accurately. With help from John and the talented researcher Juli Velazquez, we were able to interview the townspeople including the owner of the Lurancy Vennum house.

I remember arriving late at night. Upon our knock, John

greeted us politely and welcomed us into his historic home. I'm not sure if he was as excited to see us as we were him, but it was nice to finally put a face or in this case a house to the story we had been researching for months. I remember feeling dizzy, a little off balanced when we first entered. I had felt a feeling of deep remorse. The house was void from furniture and the walls were bare. An old hollow staircase beckoned me to climb, yet the parlor was the initial centerpiece calling for an investigation. In general parlors are used for receptions and formal events such as weddings, births and funerals. Yes, you guessed it. This is the room where they would show the body of the deceased.

This was how the funeral parlor got its name. It was far too morbid to call it a Death Room. The name parlor was eventually discarded when families stopped having funerals in their homes. It was then changed to living room. The ever-popular séance of that century were also held in the parlor and the Roffs' practiced this on many of occasions. This meaning we would not be alone as during séances there would be many spirits to entertain.

Our Spirit box and other form of white noise communications in this room would prove later to be scary as hell. Juli Velazquez, one of our team's paranormal investigators had caught some interesting evidence on "The Frank's Box." Invented in 2002 by Frank Sumption "The Frank's Box" is an instrumental trans-communication (ITC) device that allowed users to talk with the dead. The box sweeps radio bands and spirit voices supposedly echo through. Juli Velazquez explains;

"The first time we did the audio at the Roff house we got some very disturbing entities that seemed to be coming through the box. A lot of them were "Help me." When we asked certain things as if it was a crime an entity came over and said "Stop, that's enough." I didn't want to pursue the conversation as I felt they wanted to deter us, almost as if they had something to hide or a secret within the walls of this residence. We got approximately nineteen different types of segments that came through. Also, you have to understand that with the box you're not always hearing everything in real time. So we record everything that we do so we can go back and run through and section off each segment that comes through. And you may have more than one entity that is coming through at a time. Someone who wants to tell a story, you might also get another entity that doesn't want them to tell a story. So you can actually hear intermingling, or conversations that are transpiring back and forth on the other side."

I remember reviewing the Watseka Wonder case Electronic Voice Phenomenon back in our Los Angeles studio. There were no children at the Roff house when we recorded these EVPs as we do not allow kids on our investigations. But somehow we managed to capture the chilling voice of a young girl saying,

"Mommy why is Daddy doing this to me?"

My heart broke as I analyzed the playback. What is one's human responsibility at that point? Do you brush it under the rug of do you try and do something about it and help? It haunted me deeply, the whole investigation did. There's more than meets the eye and ear going on here. That haunting EVP was enough for me to immediately schedule another visit to the Mary Roff house and get to the bottom of what the Wonder was in Watseka.

We got over one hundred and eight EVPs. Sad, haunting unidentifiable voices of children whether at the asylum or at the house. Accompanied by Troy Taylor, Keith Age, my twin brother Philip and Bill Chappell, we set out on our final investigation. Bill of Digital Dowsing had designed some custom bio-feedback devices that would be later strapped to Psychic Medium Rick Hayes. This savvy bunch of individuals made me feel proud, as they all came together for one reason, to help get closure to one of the most extraordinary cases of possession, or was it reincarnation?

"It's one of the most unusual cases on record of spirit possession. Now three quarters of the world population believes in reincarnation. But the prevailing view is that you die and you come back into another life as an infant. Now here we have a case where a dead person stepped into the body of a young girl,"

Angel Or Devil

explained Rosemary Ellen Guiley.

We had taken Rick Hayes to the Roff house to see what he picked up.

"Immediately when I arrived there I walked up on the porch and shared with the producers, The Booth Brothers, there was a young female energy at the top of the stairs and wanted to share with us. Okay, there is a girl in here. And I am feeling that as I walked to the house she wanted me to look inside. As I looked inside she was at the top of the stairs. Don't touch this room."

The house had several bedrooms upstairs, the mother's room, the father's room and the baby's room. As we slowly walked up the rickety staircase, we stopped at the top of the stairs. There in front of us was a small green door oozing with mystery.

"Don't go there, don't go there. She was brought here." Rick said. "They thought there was something wrong with me. I didn't like this, I didn't like this at all." Rick started to feel dizzy as he closed his eyes as in a trance and quietly whispered, "Who are you?"

The house was dead silent as we all waited for the answer. "I feel like she's trying to tell me there is an "R" Rick said. "Like I don't know if that is her name. But something to do with an "R" name. A real short "R" name. She's very sad. She's very, very sad."

I probably think one of the scariest things that just blew us all away was when the bedroom door slammed. I mean, there is Rick Hayes, he just started to communicate with a spirit and suddenly the door slammed so hard it came off its hinges. Something had happened in that room and we needed to find out.

We had the great pleasure to interview Joyce Wesbrooks, the great niece of Lurancy Vennum. Now in her Eighties, she told us of her story, and her meeting of Lurancy:

"We were not ever supposed to mention it to Aunt Rancy when she visited, and we didn't. She didn't want to talk about it and be reminded of what had happened. Mother just told us that Mary Roff took over Rancy's body and that she knew things that she wouldn't ordinarily have known. I was frightened and kind of walked around her at first but we heard the story and we weren't real sure. I would think it was about possession as Lurancy went to live with the Roffs' for a time."

Now this certainly confounded people here in Watseka. Mary had been dead for 12 years and no one expected her to return. They did test her knowledge of events and things that had happened and family affairs and things. Anything they could think of. And within a few days Lurancy Vennum, or Lurancy under the power of Mary Roff, had convinced the Roff family that she was indeed their dead daughter.

It was our conclusion that Asa Roff had never reconciled

Angel Or Devil

himself to his daughter Mary's death. It was about him finally coming to terms with the fact that his daughter died. It brought release to Mary's father as he had felt a lot of guilt for having to put her in an asylum. This was her way of coming back, through Lurancy to forgive him more or less. The story became more heart breaking, when it was time for Mary Roff to leave the body of Lurancy Vennum, the Roff's' would have to lose their daughter all over again in turn watch her die twice.

IN RESPECT AND MEMORY
OF
MARY ROFF
LURANCY VENNUM

Angel Or Devil

Introduction from

THE STRANGE CASE OF THE WATSEKA WONDER

from *PARANOIA The Strange Case Of Ghosts, Demons and Aliens.*
courtesy of Spooked Productions written by Christopher Saint Booth

www.paranoiabook.com

from the documentary
THE POSSESSED
a BOOTH BROTHERS film

www.thepossessedmovie.com

featuring

THE WATSEKA WONDER STORY

Angel Or Devil

PRICE, FIFTEEN CENTS.

THE WATSEKA WONDER

A Startling and Instructive Psychological Study, and well Authenticated Instance of Angelic Visitation.

A NARRATIVE ON THE LEADING PHENOMENA OCCURRING IN THE CASE OF MARY LURANCY VENNUM,
BY E. W. STEVENS.
WITH COMMENTS RY JOSEPH RODES BUCHANAN, M.D. ANTHROPOLOGY, AND PHYSIOLOGICAL INSTITUTES OF MEDICINES IN THE ECLECTIC MEDICAL COLLEGE, NEW YORK; D. P. KAYNER, M. D. ; S. B. BRITTAN, M. D., AND HUDSON TUTTLE. CHICAGO: REL1G10-PH1LOSOPHICAL PUBLISHING HOUSE. 1878

Asterisks, spelling and grammar are included in original transcript as this journal is unedited for its accuracy.
PUBLISHERS NOTE
"Truth wears no mask, bows at no human shrine, seeks neither place nor applause: she only asks a hearing."

To members of the various learned professions we especially commend this narrative. We believe the history of the case as herein told to be strictly true. The account is given in a modest, unassuming way, with no attempt to exaggerate or enlarge; it could have been made far more thrilling and yet have remained within the bounds of truth. It will be observed there is no chance for the witnesses to have been honestly mistaken and to have thought they heard and saw that which in fact they did not. Either the account is in exact accordance with the facts or the author and witnesses have willfully prevaricated. The evidence which we publish herewith as to the credibility of the Roff family, could not be stronger; and the reputation of E. W. Stevens is equally good; the publisher has known him for years and has implicit confidence in his veracity.

    The case of Lurancy Vennum is not by any means an isolated one, and there are others which in some respects are even more remarkable. Yet on account of its recent occurrence and the facilities for investigation, we believe this case deserves and demands the careful, candid, unbiased consideration, not only of professional men, but of all who are interested, either as advocates of a future existence or as disbelievers there- in. The publisher will be glad to receive honest, intelligent criticisms, which may be
utilized in a future edition. We are all in search of truth, let us not be so blinded with prejudice as to be disgusted with its wrappings and fail to find the fair treasure so snugly ensconced within.........

                        CHICAGO, September, 1878.

THE RELIGIO-PHILOSOPHICAL JOURNAL

is a fearless and independent newspaper, entirely free from all sectarian bias. While the JOURNAL is always ready to take the affirmative side on all questions involving the phenomena and philosophy of Spiritualism, yet it demands the most stringent accuracy of observation and unhesitatingly rejects all phenomena which cannot bear the ordeal of careful scrutiny.

All Spiritualists, and those who are investigating the subject of Spiritualism, will find this paper invaluable as an assistant in their researches. The opponents of Spiritualism, who desire to be familiar with its progress and development, will find this JOURNAL a fair, candid and trustworthy channel of information.

THE WATSEKA WONDER

A Startling and Instructive Chapter in the History of Spiritualism

by E. W. STEVENS.

It was long ago and wisely said, that "God had chosen the weak things of the world to confound the wise," and that " out of the mouths of babes and sucklings, He hath perfected praise."

The innocence of childhood is often the sublimest argument in the establishment of a great truth ; and the un-presuming simplicity of youth sometimes may become the channel of phenomena calculated to shake the skepticism and prejudice of bigotry, and to humble the conceit of the pompously wise.

Such has been a fact of the last year, at the city of Watseka, a town of humble pre- tensions, on the Eastern Illinois, and Toledo, Peoria and Warsaw Railroads, eighty-six miles South of Chicago.on the Iroquois river. Watseka is noted for its orthodox sentiments and bitter animosity against all ingress of Spiritual 'ideas. Its ruling classes are aristocratic and respectable, noted for their intelligence and literary attainments. Its society organizations are earnest in reformatory measures, but the masses, like the population in all low and malarial districts, are inert in the investigation of ideas and principles, and slow in the discovery and application of truths hitherto unknown to them.

This town has been swept by a tidal wave of excitement, on account of the presumed insanity of one Lurancy Vennum, a young girl belonging to an unpretentious family in the suburbs of the city. Her insanity, as it was thought to be, dates from July ll, 1877, and the remarkable phenomenon continued until her perfect restoration through the aid of friendly Spiritualists and spirits, on the 21st of May, 1878.

Thus, for ten months and ten days, did these phenomena continue to excite and agitate the people. The following is a true narrative, and as full as the facts collected from the parents and relatives of the parties named herein and observations made by the writer, will warrant.

Thomas J. Vennum was born May 7th, 1832, in Washington Co., Penn.; Lurinda J. Smith (his wife), was born October 14th, 1837, in St. Joseph Co., Ind. They were married in Fayette Co., Iowa, Dec. 2nd, 1855.

MARY LURANCY VENNUM,

daughter of the above named Thomas J. and Lurinda J. Vennum, was born on the 16th day of April, 1864, in Milford township, seven miles south of Watseka. The family moved to Iowa, July, 12th, 1864, and returned to the vicinity eight miles from Watseka, in Oct., 1865. In August, 1866, they removed to Milford, twelve miles south of Watseka, and remained there till March 1st, 1870, then moved out two and one-half miles from Milford until April 1st, 1871, when they moved into Watseka, locating about forty rods from the residence of A. B. Roff, the spirit daughter of whom, according to all the facts and representations every way tested, is the principal character in this remarkable narrative. The family remained at this place during the summer. The only acquaintance ever had between the two families during the season, was simply one brief call of Mrs. Roff, for a few minutes, on Mrs. Vennum, which call was never returned and a formal speaking acquaintance between the two gentlemen. Since 1871, the Vennum family have lived entirely away from the vicinity of Mr. Roff's, and never nearer than now, on extreme opposite limits of the city.

"Rancy," as she is familiarly called, had never been sick, save a light run of measles in 1873. A few days before the following incidents took place, she said to her family : "*There were persons in my room last night, and they called 'Rancy I Rancy I' and I felt their breath on my face.*" The very next night she arose from her bed, saying that she could not sleep, that every time she tried to sleep, persons came and called *"Rancy! Rancy!"* to her. Her mother went to bed with her, after which she rested and slept the rest of the night.

On the eleventh day of July, 1877, Lurancy had been sewing carpet a part of the afternoon, when, at about six o'clock she laid by her work, as her mother said : *"Lurancy, you had better commence getting supper."* The girl replied : *"Ma, I feel bad; I feel so queer,"* and placing her hand to her left breast, she immediately went into what seemed like a fit, falling heavily on the floor, lying apparently dead, every muscle becoming suddenly rigid. Thus she lay five hours. On returning to consciousness she said she felt *"very strange and queer."* The remainder of the night she rested well. The next day the rigid state returned, and passing beyond the rigidity, her mind took cognizance of two states of being at the same time. Lying as if dead, she spoke freely, telling the family what persons and spirits she could see, describing them and calling some of them by name. Among those mentioned were her sister and brother, for she exclaimed, *"Oh, mother! can't you see little Laura and Bertie? They are so beautiful!"* etc., etc. Bertie died when Lurancy was but three years old.

She had many of these trances, describing Heaven and the spirits, or the angels as she called them. Sometime in September she became free from them and seemed to the family to be quite well again.

On the 27th day of November, 1877, she was attacked with a most violent pain in her stomach, some five or six times a day ; for two weeks she had the most excruciating pains. In these painful paroxysms, she would double herself back until her head and feet actually touched. At the end of two weeks, or about the eleventh of December, in these distressed attacks, she became unconscious and passed into a quiet trance, and, as at former times, would describe Heaven and spirits, often calling them angels.

From this time on until the 1st of February, 1878, she would have these trances and sometimes a seemingly real obsession, from three to eight and sometimes as many as twelve times a day, lasting from one to eight hours, occasionally passing into that state of ecstasy, when, as Lurancy, she claimed to be in heaven.

During the time recorded, up to about the middle of

January 1878, she had been under the care of Dr. L. N. Pitwood in the summer and Dr. Jewett during the winter. These M. D.'s are both eminent allopathic practitioners, and residents of Watseka. Mrs. Allison, Mrs. Jolly and other relatives and friends believed her insane. The Rev. B. M. Baker, the Methodist minister in charge at Watseka, wrote to the insane asylum to ascertain if the girl could be received there. It seemed to be the general feeling among all the friends, save the parents and a few who were only sympathetic observers and thinkers, that the girl should taken from to the asylum.

There were in the city of Watseka at this time, persons who had more humanity than bigotry; persons who believe, in the language of Bishop A. Beals, that "disease has a dynamic or spiritual origin;" persons claiming to understand something of the occult forces and phenomena of mind, and the diseases incident to a false conception of, and opposition to, its potencies; persons who believe, God being "no respecter of persons " and "without variableness or shadow of turning," that power exists to-day, as in the days of the Nazarene, to cast out devils. Among this class were Asa B. Roff and his wife, who, with others, became thoroughly aroused to the importance of arresting the movement, to take a lovely child from the home of an affectionate family, to imprison her among maniacs, to be ruled and cared for by ignorant and bigoted strangers, who know less of catalepsy than a blind materialist does of immortality. These good people ventured in the most gentle and Christian spirit, to counsel with the parents and advise other treatment, different from any that had been administered.

These earnest, self-sacrificing souls, imbued with the conviction that uncultivated spirits had something to do with the case, plead with the many friends of the child, to withhold her from the asylum until it could be better shown whether the girl was really insane, or her unfortunate condition might be attributable to foreign minds.

Mr. Roff, after much persuasion, obtained the consent of the girl's father, to visit her and bring with him Dr. E. W. Stevens, of Janesville Wis., to investigate the case. Dr. Stevens, who, for several months, at frequent intervals, had been in the city and a silent listener to the scoffs and scandals thrown out toward the Spiritualists on account of their opinions regarding the case, and the universal foment of mind in the city over it, was formally invited by Mr. Vennum, through Mr. Roff, to visit the family.

On the afternoon of January 31st, 1878, the two gentlemen repaired to Mr. Vennum's residence, a little out of the city. Dr. Stevens, an entire stranger to the family, was introduced by Mr. Roff at four o'clock PM ; no other persons present but the family.

Angel Or Devil

The girl sat near the stove, in a common chair, her elbows on her knees, her hands under her chin, feet curled up on the chair, eyes staring, looking every way like an "old hag." She sat for a time in silence, until Dr. Stevens moved his chair, when she savagely warned him not to come nearer. She appeared sullen and crabbed, calling her father *"Old Black Dick, and her mother "Old Granny."* She refused to be touched, even to shake hands, and was reticent and sullen with all save the doctor, with whom she entered freely in conversation, giving her reasons for doing so ; she said he was a Spiritual doctor and would understand her. When he asked her name she quickly replied:

"Katrina Hogan."
"How old?"
"Sixty-three years."
"Where from?"
"Germany."
"How long ago ? "
"Three days."
"How did you come? "
"Through the air."
"How long will you stay?"
"Three weeks."

Angel Or Devil

After this system of conversation had proceeded for some time, she modified her manners very much, appearing to be a little penitent and confidential.and said she would be honest and tell the doctor her real name. She was not a woman; and her real name was Willie. On being asked what was her father's name, replied, *" Peter Canning, and her own name was Willie Canning, a young man; ran away from home, got into difficulty, changed his name several times and finally lost his life and was now here because he wanted to be,"* etc. She wearied with answering questions and giving details. Then she turned upon the doctor with a perfect shower of questions, such as,

"What is your name ?
Were do you live ?
Are you married?
How many children?
How many boys ?
How many girls ?
What is your occupation ?
What kind of a doctor ?
What did you come to Watseka for ?
Have you ever been at the South Pole ? North Pole ?
Europe ? Australia? Egypt? Ceylon? Benares ? Sandwich Islands ? "

and by along series of questions evinced a knowledge of geography. She next inquired after the doctor's habits and morals by questions like the following:

"Do you lie ? get drunk ? steal ? swear ? use tobacco? tea? coffee? Do you go to church? pray ? " etc., etc.

She then asked to have the same questions put Mr. Roff. She declined to ask them direct, herself, but through the doctor. They must also be repeated through him to Mr. Vennum, making: the while, some very unpleasant retorts.

When, at about half-past five o'clock, the visitors arose to depart, she also arose, flung up her hands and fell upon the floor, straight, stiff and rigid, as I have often seen sensitives fall with the " power" in Methodist revival meetings, and believing it to be of the same nature, the doctor took occasion to prove it, as he has done on those smitten with the "power," by controlling body and mind and restoring them to a normal and rational state, despite the " power."

The visitors being again seated, he took her hands as they were held straight upwards, like iron bars, and by magnetic action soon had the body under perfect control, and through the laws of Spiritual science, was soon in full and free communication with the sane and happy mind of Lurancy Vennum herself, who conversed with, the grace and sweetness of an angel, declaring herself to be in heaven.

In this condition she answered the doctor's questions with reference to herself, her seemingly insane condition and the influences that controlled her, with great rationality and understanding. She regretted to have such evil controls about her. She said she knew the evil spirit calling itself Katrina and Willie and others. The doctor continued to suggest to her mind, things to prepare the way for a change of influences, by enlightening and instructing her no while her mind was clear and in this superior condition, and then asked her, if she must be controlled, if it would not be better, if it were possible, to have a higher, purer, happier, and more intelligent or rational control. She said she would rather, if it could be so. Then on being advised, she looked about and inquired of those she saw, and described, and named, to find some one who would prevent the cruel and insane ones from returning to annoy her and the family. She soon said: *"There are a great many spirits here who would be glad to come,"* and she again proceeded to give names and descriptions of persons long since deceased ; some that she had never known, but were known by older persons present. But, she said, there is one the angels desire should come, and she wants to come. On being asked if she knew who it was, she said: *"Her name is Mary Roff."* Mr. Kofi being present, said:

Angel Or Devil

"That is my daughter ; Mary Roff is my girl. Why, she has been in heaven twelve years. Yes, let her come, we'll be glad to have her come." Mr. Roff assured Lurancy that Mary was good and intelligent and would help her all she could; stating further that Mary used to be subject to conditions like herself. Lurancy, after due deliberation and counsel with spirits, said that Mary would take the place of the former wild and unreasonable influence. Mr. Roff said to her: *"Have your mother bring you to my house and Mary will be likely to come along, and a mutual benefit may be derived from our former experience with Mary."* Thus reaching the sane mind of the girl and through her, the sane minds of a better class of spirits, a contract or agreement was made, to be kept sacred by the angels in Heaven and Heaven's agents in the flesh, by which a mortal body was to be restored to health ; a spirit, unfortunate in earth life, with twelve years' experience in spirit life, to have an amended earthly experience, a child to be spiritualized and moulded into a fine medium, an unbelieving and scoffing city to be confounded, and the greatest truth the world has ever sought, established beyond doubt or cavil. How far the contract has been kept by the spirits and their faithful co-laborers here, the sequel will show.

The object of the visit now being attained. Dr. Stevens asked :

Angel Or Devil

"How long do you want to stay in this heaven?"
She answered.
"Always sir."
"But you will come back for the sake of your friends?"
"Yes, sir."
"When will you come back?"
"At twelve o'clock."
"But the family will want rest. Can't you come sooner?"
"Yes, sir, I can."
"How soon can you come?"
"At nine o'clock, sir."
"Will you come at nine?"
"I will."

And so she did.

After nearly three hours of careful investigation, conversation, and the application of the laws of Spiritual science and harmony, Mr. Roff and the doctor retired, leaving the family satisfied that a new fountain of light and source of help had been reached. A new beam of truth reached and touched the hearts of the sorrowing family, and to use the language of Mary Roff, *"Dr. Stevens opened the gate for her,"* and for the inflowing of light where before was darkness.

Angel Or Devil

On the following morning, Friday, Feb. 1st, Mr. Vennum called at the office of Mr. Roff and informed him that the girl claimed to be Mary Roff and wanted to go home. To use Mr. Vennum's words : *"She seems like a child real home sick, wanting to see her pa and ma and her brothers."*

It now becomes necessary in the relation of this narrative to give a brief sketch of the life of MARY ROFF.

The daughter of Asa B. and Ann Roff, was born on the 8th day of October, 1846, in Warren Co., Ind. The family moved in Nov. of the same year to Williamsport, Ind., thence in September, 1847, to Middleport, Ill., where they resided till June, 1857, when they removed to Victoria, Texas, in search of relief for a sick child. In March, 1858, they returned to Gilman and remained there and at Onarga, till the building of the Toledo, Peoria and Warsaw Railroad, when they returned to Middleport, Nov. 5th, 1859 and built the first house in the new town of South Middleport, which is now a part of the city of Watseka, where they still reside.

In the spring of 1847, when about six months old, Mary was taken sick and had a fit, in which she remained several hours. After the fit, she became conscious and lay several days without the family having much hope of her recovery. In two or three weeks she seemed to have entirely recovered. A few weeks later she acted, on one occasion, like a child going into a fit. The pupils of her eyes dilated, the muscles slightly twitched but lasted but a few moments. From the age of about six months, she had these spells as described, once in from three to five weeks apart, all the time increasing in force and violence, until her tenth year, when they proved to be real fits, having from one to three and sometimes four or five of them within a period of three or four days, when they would cease, and she would enjoy good health until the next period approached. At these times, she for few days would seem sad and despondent, in which mood she would sing and play the most solemn music, (for with all the rest of her studies, in which she was considered well advanced, she had learned music,) and almost always would sing that beautiful song, "We Are Coming Sister Mary," which was a favorite song with her.

When she was fifteen years old, and the violence of the fits had increased, the parents say they could see her mind was affected during the melancholy periods prior to the fits. Dr. Jesse Bennett, now residing at Sparta, Wis., and Dr. Franklin Blades, now Judge of the Eleventh Judicial Circuit of Illinois, and resident of Watseka, were employed to attend her. Dr.N. S. Davis, of Chicago, Illinois, and several other prominent physicians, had examined her. They kept her in the water cure at Peoria, Illinois, under the care of Dr. Nevins, for eighteen months, but all to no purpose.

In the summer of 1864 she seemed to have almost a mania

for bleeding herself for the relief, as she said, "of the lump of pain in the head." Drs. Fowler, Secrest and Pitwood were called and applied leeches. She would apply them herself to her temples, and liked them, treating them like little pets, until she seemed sound and well.

On Saturday morning, July 16th, 1864, in one of her desponding moods, she secretly took a knife with her to the back yard, and cut her arm terribly, until bleeding excessively, she fainted. This occurred about nine o'clock A. M. She remained unconscious till two o'clock P. M., when she became a raving maniac of the most violent kind, in which condition she remained five days and nights, requiring almost constantly the services of five of the most able bodied men to hold her on the bed, although her weight was only about one hundred pounds, and she had lost nearly all her blood. When she ceased raving, she looked and acted quite natural and well, and could do everything she desired as readily and properly as at any time in her life. Yet she seemed to know no-one, and could not recognize the presence of persons at all, although the' house was nearly filled with people night and day. She had no sense whatever of sight, feeling or hearing in a natural way, as was proved by every test that could be applied. She could read blind-folded, and do everything as readily as when in health by her natural sight. She would dress, stand before the glass, open and search drawers, pick up loose pins, or do any and all things readily, and without annoyance under heavy blind-foldings.

Near the time, in 1864, when she cut her arm while blindfolded, she took Dr. Trail's encyclopedia, turned to the index, traced the column till she came to the word "blood," then turned to the page indicated and read the subject through. On another occasion she took a box of her letters received from her friends, and sat down, heavily blindfolded by critical, intelligent, investigating gentlemen, examined and read them without error or hesitancy. When Rev. J. H. Rhea, Editor A. J. Smith, Mr. Roff and others misplaced and promiscuously arranged some of their own letters with Mary s, she at once proceeded to correctly draw out the intruded letters and examine them. If wrong side up, she would quickly turn them, and read aloud the address thereon, and throw violently away every letter not her own; and re-arranged twenty or thirty letters in the order she desired to have them. Rev. J. H. Rhea was the Methodist minister in charge at that time ; A. G. Smith was editor of the Iroquois county Republican, now editor of the Danville (Ill.) Times. She was also investigated by all the prominent citizens of Watseka at that time.

With the physicians her peculiar state or condition was called catalepsy. With the clergy it was one of the mysteries of God's providence, with which we should have little to do. With editors, who are obliged to be wise or silent, it was fits or some unaccountable phenomenon. All, with untiring effort, tried to solve the mystery, and learn what it was that produced such strange and wonderful manifestations. The editor of the *Danville Times*, in a recent issue writes :

"Now as to Mary Roff, it was our fortune to know the sweet girl, who was cataleptic, and who died twelve years ago. Disease dethroned her reason and maddened her brain until she sought her own and others' lives, and the modest young lady was transformed into a screaming maniac. She had periods of exemption from raving, and thus her aberrant mind conceived fancies of the queerest hue, creating the most impossible beings for associates, and conversing with them, she maintained her own side of the conversation in a usual tone of voice, while imagination supplied her created associates with language and intelligence. When in this condition, her father and mother asserted the discovery that Mary could read a book with its lids closed, and they desired us to test the correctness of what they claimed. We therefore took from our side pocket a letter inclosed in an envelope, and holding it before her bandaged eyes, said to her, 'Mary, read the signature to that letter.' Immediately the proper name was pronounced."

After remaining in the clairvoyant state above related for three or four days, she came again to her normal condition and in good health as she usually was, except the fits. From this time she continued as she had been prior to cutting her arm. Her fits increased, and her parents were advised to place her in the insane asylum.

On July 5th, 1865, while her parents were at Peoria, Illinois, on a three days' visit, she ate a hearty breakfast, and soon thereafter lay down on her bed, and in her usual health went to sleep. In a few minutes she was heard to scream, as was usual on taking a a fit. On approaching her bedside, they found her in a fit, and in a few moments she expired.

We now return and take up the original narrative where we left it, dating Feb. 1st, 1878, when it was first seen that Mary Roff had control of Lurancy's body, and teasing to go home. Could it be possible the gulf of death had been bridged I the gates of heaven left open ? Had Mary, like Moses and Elias, returned to a transfiguration ? Or, like the spirit of "one of the prophets," had she come with revelation to the grotto of darkness in this benighted Patmos ? Were the unnumbered facts of scriptural ages repeating themselves now ? Can we say with Job, *"A spirit passed before my face?"* Ezekiel and Isaiah talked with the departed, Saul conversed with Samuel, Paul and the shepherds with spirits in the air, and can we talk with Mary ? And the friends of the family went up to see, and answered, *"Yes!"*

Angel Or Devil

From the wild, angry, ungovernable girl, to be kept only by lock and key, or the more distressing watch care of almost frantic parents; or the rigid, corpse-like cataleptic, as believed, the girl has now become mild, docile, polite and timid, knowing none of the family, but constantly pleading to go home. The best wisdom of the family was used to convince her that she was at home, and must remain. Weeping, she would not be pacified, and only found contentment in going back to heaven, as she said, for short visits.

About a week after she took control of the body, Mrs. A. B. Roff and her daughter, Mrs. Minerva Alter, Mary's sister, hear- ing of the remarkable change, went to see the girl. As they came in sight, far down the street) Mary, looking out the window, exclaimed exultingly, *"There comes my ma and sister Nervie!"* the name by which Mary used to call Mrs. Alter in girlhood. As they came into the house, she caught them around their necks, wept and cried for joy, and seemed so happy to meet them. From this time on she seemed more homesick than before. At times she seemed almost frantic to go home. Finally some friends of the family insisted on their sending her to Mr. Roffs, which they reluctantly consented to do; reluctantly because the girl was so much trouble and care as she had been all winter; so much so that Mrs. Vennum was nearly prostrated, and could not have survived the care and anxiety many months longer, under the same state of affairs, and they felt that it would be an imposition to send the girl to be cared for by strangers and especially so by Mrs. Roff, as she was not able to take charge of and care for a girl that made so much trouble as this one had for Mrs. Vennum.

Mr. and Mrs. Roff, with their hearts ever full of the milk of human kindness, more ready to forgive than to censure, and braving the sneers and taunting innuendoes of an uneducated bigotry, with no other motive but one of mercy and kindness, opened their doors and hearts to receive the unfortunate girl with her new control, having no hope or desire for reward but in the sense of a just sympathy for right and truth. They remembered the precept, "Forget not to entertain strangers, for thereby some have entertained angels."

On the 11th day of February, 1878, they sent the girl to Mr. Roff's, where she met her "pa and ma," and each member of the family, with the most gratifying expressions of love and affection, by words and embraces. On being asked how long she would stay, she said, *"The angels will let me stay till some time in May ;"* and she made it her home there till May 21st, three months and ten days, a happy, contented daughter and sister in a borrowed body.

After the girl was at Mr. Roff's, the Rev. Mr. Baker said to Mr. Vennum, *"I think you will see the time when you will wish you had sent her to the asylum."* Mrs. Jolly said if she ever came home she would be more trouble than ever. Another relative, more religious than humane, said, *"I would sooner follow a girl of mine to the grave than have her go to Roff's and be made a Spiritualist."* Dr. Jewett called it catalepsy No. 2, which is as definite and convenient in explanation of this case as is "humbug" in explanation of any newly discovered scientific truth unacceptable to popular ignorance. He said : *"Humor her whims and she will get well."* Some *prudent, two-faced people would say, with a noncommittal air, "What strange freaks!" Others, with an exalted opinion of their wonderful perceptions, would say, "It is all put on,"* etc., etc.

Yet none of the persons expressing such opinions have ever called to see the girl, or derived any information from those in charge of her.

The girl now in her new home, seemed perfectly happy and content, knowing every person and everything that Mary knew when in her original body, twelve to twenty-five years ago, recognizing and calling by name those who were friends and neighbors of the family from 1852 to 1865, when Mary died, calling attention to scores, yes hundreds, of incidents that transpired during her natural life. During all the period of her sojourn at Mr. Roff's she had no knowledge of, and did not recognize any of Mr. Vennum's family, their friends or neighbors, yet Mr. and Mrs. Vennum and their children visited her and Mr. Roff's people, she being introduced to them as to any strangers. After frequent visits, and hearing them often and favorably spoken of, she learned to love them as acquaintances, and visited them with Mrs. Roff three times. From day to day she appeared natural, easy, affable and industrious, attending diligently and faithfully to her household duties, assisting in the general work of the family as a faithful, prudent daughter might be supposed to do, singing, reading or conversing as opportunity offered, upon all matters of private or general interest to the family.

Three days after she came to Mr. Roff's, while looking at him and seeming to have been in a sort of retrospective revery, she asked, *"Pa, who was it that used to say 'confound it?"* and laughing very heartily when she saw that he understood it to be himself, that being a common expression of his in the time of her girlhood, twelve to twenty years ago.

One day she met an old friend and neighbor of Mr. Roff's, who was a widow when Mary was a girl at home. Some years since, he lady married a Mr. Wagoner with whom he yet lives. But when she met Mrs. Wagner she clasped her around the neck, and said, *"Mary Lord, you look so very natural, and have changed the least of any one I have seen since I came back."*

Angel Or Devil

Mrs. Lord was in some way related to the Vennum family, and lived close by them, but Mary could only call her by the name by which she knew her fifteen years ago, and could not seem to realize that she was married. Mrs. Lord lived just across the street from Mr. Roff s for several years, prior and up to within a few months of Mary's death ; both being members of the same Methodist church, they were very intimate.

Some days after Mary was settled in her new home, Mrs. Parker, who lived neighbor to the Roff's in Middleport in 1852, and next door to them in Watseka in 1860, came in with her daughter-in-law, Nellie Parker. Mary immediately recognized both of the ladies, calling Mrs. Parker "Auntie Parker," and the other "Nellie," as in the acquaintance of eighteen years ago. In conversation with Mrs. Parker, Mary asked, *"Do you remember how Nervie and I used to come to your house and sing?"* Mrs. Parker says that was the first allusion made to that matter, nothing having been said by any one on that subject, and says that Mary and Minerva used to come to their house and sit and sing, "Mary had a little lamb,"etc. Mrs. Dr. Alter (Minerva) says she remembers it well. This was when Mr Roff kept the postoffice, and could not have been later than 1852, and twelve years before Lurancy was born.

One evening in the latter part of March, Mr. Roff was sitting in the room waiting for tea, and reading the paper, Mary being out in the yard. He asked Mrs. Roff if she could find a certain velvet head-dress that Mary used to wear the last year before she died. If so, to lay it on the stand and say nothing about it, to see if Mary would recognize it. Mrs. Roff readily found and laid it on the stand. The girl soon came in, and immediately exclaimed as she approached the stand :

"O, there is my head-dress I wore when my hair was short !" She then asked, *"Ma, where is my box of letters ? Have you got them yet?"* Mrs. Roff replied, *"Yes, Mary, I have some of them."* She at once got the box with many letters in it. *As Mary began to examine them she said, O, "Ma here is a collar I tatted! Ma, why, did you not show to me my letters and things before?"*

The collar had been preserved among the relics of the lamented child as one of the beautiful things her fingers had wrought before Lurancy was born ; and so Mary continually recognized every little thing and remembered every little incident of her girlhood.

It will be remembered that the family moved to Texas in 1857. Mr. Roff asked Mary if she remembered moving to Texas or anything about it. *"Yes, pa, and I remember crossing the river and of seeing a great many Indians, and I remember Mrs. Eeeder's girls, who were in our company,"* and other incidents and facts. And thus she from time to time made first mention of things that transpired thirteen to twenty five years ago.

On the 19th of February Mr. Roff addressed the writer as follows : "You know how we took the poor, dear girl Lurancy (Mary). Some appreciate our motives, but the many, without investigation and without a knowledge of the facts, cry out against us and against that angel girl. Some say she pretends; others that she is crazy; and we hear that some say it is the devil. * * * Mary is perfectly happy ; she recognizes everybody and everything that she knew when in her body twelve or more years ago. She knows nobody nor anything whatever that is known by Lurancv. * * * Mr. Vennum has been to see her, and also her brother Henry, at different times, but she don't know anything about them. Mrs. Vennum is still unable to come and see her daughter. She has been nothing but Mary since she has been here, and knows nothing but what Mary knew. She has entered the trance once every other day for some days. She is perfectly happy. * * * You don't know how much comfort we take with the dear angel."

The child has often said she likes Dr Stevens next to her pa, because he opened the gate for her to come in, and because he has done so much for her pa and ma, and her brothers, and for Lurancy's body, and feeling that gratitude, she wrote him by permission of the parents, on the 20th of February, in which she said:

"I am yet here. * * * Frank is better." * * Nervie is

here for dinner ; Allie Alter is going to stay all night; Mrs. Marsh was here to-day and read a beautiful letter to us. I wish you could spend the evening with us. * I would like to have your picture to look at. * * Please write to pa when you get time. * * We all send our love to you. * * I like it here very much, and am going to stay all the time. * * * I went to heaven and staid about an hour. * It seems a long time since I saw you. Forget me not. Good night.

MARY ROFF.

She wrote the doctor again in February of which the following is an extract:

"I have just finished a letter to brother Frank. He went back to his store feeling quite well. The boys have gone put to play for a dance. In the evening I went to heaven, and I saw some of the beautiful things, and talked with the angels, * * * and be sure 1 don't forget when I go to heaven and come back.

'Fear the Lord and depart from evil' -Prov.3d:7th.

MARY ROFF.

It may here be said that it was frequently the case that when Mary went to heaven, as she called it, other spirits sometimes, by permission, would come and pre- sent themselves, and speak freely their own language and sentiments. Mr. Roff writes under date of

Angel Or Devil

March, as follows, of a communication through another young lady at his house. The medium's name I reserve because I have no license to use it :

"A lady came through ---- at our house, who claimed to have lived and died in Tennessee, and says she was afflicted from eight years of age till twenty-five, when she died with a similar disease, and in a similar way that Mary died. She says that Mary has control or Lurancy Vennum, and will retain control till she is restored to her normal condition, when Mary will leave. Mary is happy as a lark, and gives daily, almost hourly, proofs of being Mary's intelligence. She don't recognize Lurancy's family or friends at all. She knows and recognizes everything that our Mary used to know, and nothing whatever of what the Vennum girl knows. She now enters the trance without any rigidity of the muscles whatever, very gently, and at her own will, describes heavenly scenes, etc., etc. We think all will be well, and Lurancy restored to her orthodox friends yet. * * Some of the relatives are yielding by Mary's calling their attention to things of thirteen years ago, that transpired between her and them. It wakes them up. * * It is wonderful. * * It would take a volume to give the important items that have occurred."

Mrs. Dr. Alter, under date of April 16th, 1878, writes of Mary as follows:

"My angel sister says she is going away from us again

soon, but says she will be often with us. She says Lurancy is a beautiful girl ; says she sees her nearly every day, and we do know she is getting better every day. Oh, the lessons that are being taught us are worth treasures of rare diamonds ; they are stamped upon the mind so firmly that heaven and earth shall pass away before one jot or one tittle shall be forgotten. * * * I have learned so much that is grand and beautiful, I cannot express it ; I am dumb. * * A few days ago Mary was caressing her father and mother, and they became a little tired of it, and asked why she hugged and kissed them. She sorrowfully looked at them, and said, 'Oh, pa and ma! I want to kiss you while I have lips to kiss you with, and hug you while I have arms to hug you with, for I am going back to heaven before long, and then I can only be with you in spirit, and you will not always know when I come, and I cannot love you as I can now. Oh, how much I love you all"

Mary writes to Dr. Stevens, in an envelope with Mr. Roff, under date of May 7th, as follows :

DEAR DOCTOR:
I thought I would write you. I am at Aunt Carrie's ; am going to take dinner with her. * * Yesterday I went and spent the day with Mrs. Vennum. She had a dreadful headache and I rubbed it away. Pa is quite busy in his office to-day. Ma is

feeling a good deal better. * * Iam feeling quite well, except my breast hurts me some to-day. It commenced hurting me last night. * * I treat ma in the morning and Nervie at night for hard colds and cold feet. "We all went to the Reform Club last Saturday. Aunt Carrie's essay was splendid, and very affecting, * * We all read that letter in the RELIGIO-PHILOSOPHICAL JOURNAL from your daughter, and liked it.

MARY ROFF.

In the same letter Mr. Roff writes:

"I want to give you a little scene ; time, Monday moraine:, May 6th; place, A. B. Roff's office, Watseka; present, A. B. Roff at table writing; Frank Roff at the table at the right or A. B. R. ; door behind A. B., and a little to the left; enters unheard the person of Lurancy Vennum ; places her arm around the neck of A. B. Roff, kissing him and saying, 'Pa I am going with Mrs. Vennum to visit to-day ; ' A. B. Roff looks around and discovers standing in the door Mrs. Vennum, Lurancv 'smother, looking on the scene. The girl then bade an affectionate good-by to Frank ; A. B. R. asks : 'How long will you stay ? ' She replies, 'Till two or three or o'clock.' Mrs. Vennum then said to Mr. Roff : 'If she does not get back at that time, don't get alarmed, we will take care of her.' Exit Mrs. V. and the girl. You don't know how my heart aches for that poor mother, yet she is much happier than she was last

Angel Or Devil

winter with Lurancy as she was." * *

On May 7th, the day of writing the last letter, Mary called Mrs. Roff to a private room, and there in tears told her that Lurancy Vennum was coming back. She seemed very sad, and said she could not tell whether she was coming to stay or not ; that if she thought she was coming to stay, she would want to see Nervie and Dr. Alter and Allie, and bid them good-by. She sat down, closed her eyes and in a few moments the change took place, and Lurancy had control of her own body. Looking wildly around the room she anxiously asked :

"Where am I ? I was never here before."

Mrs. Roff replied.

"No, but Mary did." "You are at Mr. Roff's, brought here by Mary to cure your body."

She cried and said :

"I want to go home."

Mrs. Roff asked her if she could stay till her folks were sent for. She said : *"No."*

She was then asked if she felt any pain in her breast. (This was during the period that Mary was suffering pain in the left breast ; continually holding her hand, pressing it.) She replied :

"No, but Mary did."

In about five minutes the change was again made, and

Mary came overjoyed to find herself permitted to return, and called, as she often had, for the singing of her previous girlhood's favorite song, "We are Coming Sister Mary."

The child seemed possessed of all the natural affection for the family that a daughter and sister of fine feelings and cultivated tastes might be supposed to possess, after an absence of twelve years, and she often took occasion to demonstrate that affection by endearing names and kindly words. When walking with Mrs. Alter, her sister Nervie as she called her, she would say, *"Nervie, my only sister, put your arm around me." Or, "Come Nervie, put your arm around me and we will take a little walk in the garden or the grove, for I cannot be with you much longer and I want to be with you every minute I can."* When Mrs. Alter would ask her when or where she was going, she would say *"The angels tell me I am going to heaven, but I don't know just when. O, how I wish you could live here at home with us as you used to when I was here before."* She thought a great deal of Dr. Alter, the husband of her sister, but could hardly seem realize that Nervie was married and had a family for eleven years. She said when she got into this body she felt much as she did when she was here twelve years ago. This body seemed as natural to her as though she had been born with it, yet she would not do with it as she would like to. She did not seem to realize at first, but this was her own original, physical body, until angels explained it to her. and she had received information and instructions from her parents, sister,brother and friends about it. So natural did it seem to her, after knowing all the facts, that she could hardly feel it was not her original body born nearly thirty years ago.

In conversation with the writer about her former life, she spoke of cutting her arm as heretofore stated, and asked if he ever saw where she did it. On receiving a negative answer, she proceeded to slip up her sleeve as if to exhibit the scar, but suddenly arrested the movement, as if by a sudden thought, and quickly said, *"This is not the arm ; that one is in the ground,"* and proceeded to tell where it was buried, and how she saw it done and who stood around, how they felt, etc., but she did not feel bad. I heard her tell Mr. Roff and the friends present, how she wrote to him a message some years ago through the hand of a medium, giving name, time and place. Also of rapping and of spelling out a message by another medium, giving time, name, place, etc., etc., which the parents admitted to be all true. I heard her relate a story of her going into the country with the men, some twenty odd years ago, after a load of hay, naming incidents that occurred on the road, which two of the gentlemen distinctly remembered.

In one of those beautiful trances which rendered her entirely oblivious to all physical surroundings, appearing in a state of happy ecstasy, and, so far as manners and movements are concerned, perfectly normal and graceful, with visions and senses fully open, she went to heaven as she called it, in company with another young lady in like condition, whose name must be reserved until the wonderful history she is making, shall be made public by the consent of all. They saw and conversed about the beautiful scenes before them, pointing out individuals, giving names, relationship, histories facts, etc., describing places and things. Mary pointed out and described some with titles of Royalty, such as Mary Queen of Scotts, Henry IV, King of France, and others of equal note, showing a rich biographical and historical reading or experience and acquaintance in spirit-life. Then bowing low, and kneeling with hands folded, and heads together, as if in the most devout and solemn devotion remained in listening silence for some time, then rising, the unnamed girl said :

"He came to bless, didn't he Mary? a bright, beautiful, angel."

After talking of the different classes they were observing, and the "lovely children" attracting so much of their attention, Mary seemed to take in her arms a very little, tender infant and said: *"This is Sister Nervie's baby ; how sweet and beautiful it is. Don't you think it is a sweet little angel?"* The other, in softest accents said, *"Yes, but it seems to me they are all too pure to be touched by such as we,"* and after some time the babe was carefully handed back to the care of the angels. Mrs. Alter, who was present, had recently lost by death, a beautiful babe and had scarcely recovered from her confinement. The whole scene was one of uncommon interest, very affecting and impressive beyond description.

For the discovery of facts unknown to others, Mary seemed remarkably developed. One afternoon, she, with much concern and great anxiety, declared that her brother Frank must be carefully watched the coming night, for he would be taken very sick, and would die if not properly cared for. At the time of this announcement he was in his usual health, and engaged with the Roff Bros.' band of music up town. The same evening, Dr. Stevens had been in to see the family, and on leaving, was to go directly to Mrs. Hawks, far off in the Old Town, and the family so understood it. But at about nine and a half o'clock the same evening, Dr. Stevens returned unannounced to Mr. Marsh's, Mr. Roff's next neighbor, for the night. At two o'clock in the morning Frank was attacked with something like a spasm and congestive chill, which almost destroyed his consciousness. Mary at once saw the situation as predicted, and said,

"Send to Mrs. Marsh's for Dr. Stevens. "No, Dr. Stevens is at Old Town," said the family. "No," said Mary, "he is at Mr.

Angel Or Devil

Marsh's ; go quick for him, pa."

Mr. Roff called, and the doctor, as Mary said, was at Mr. Marsh's. On his arrival at the sick bed, Mary had entire control of the case. She had made Mrs. Roff set down ; had provided hot water and cloths and other necessaries, and was doing all that could be done for Frank. The doctor seconded her efforts and allowed her to continue. She saved her brother, but never made a move after the doctor's arrival, with out his co-operation or advice.

Mary often spoke of seeing the children of Dr. Stevens in heaven, who were about her age and of longer residence there than herself. She said she was with them much, and went to his home with him. She correctly described his home, the rooms, furniture, gave names and ages of his children, and as evidence of her truthfulness, told of a remarkable experience of Mrs. E. M. Wood, one of the doctor's married daughters, which, on account of its peculiar features, and the faith of some of the relatives was not intended for the public, yet was a beautiful evidence of angel guardianship. She stated the story minutely, saying that was where and when she got Mrs. "Woods' name, for she was present with others she named.

The doctor's daughter Emma Angelia, who had been in spirit-life since March 10th, 1849, sought through Mary to take the body she was controlling and go home with her father to

Wisconsin, to visit the family for a week, and Mary was disposed to let her do it ; she asked Mr. and Mrs. Roff if she should let Emma Stevens have the body for a week to go with her father to see and be with her mother, sisters and brother, so they could realize it was Emma ? But no one thought it advisable.

To show the ease with which Mary controls, or goes in and out, as it is said, and the perfect medium the body of Lurancy is, a single instance will suffice. On the 21st day of April, in the parlors of Mrs. Roff, in the presence of Mr. and Mrs. Roff, their hired woman Charlotte, Doctor Steel and wife, Mrs. Twing, of Oregon, Mrs. Alter, Mr. and Mrs. ------- , and the writer, manifestations of a very peculiar and happy character occurred. Mary being the last one to join the company in the parlor, took the only vacant seat, next a gentleman friend. Dr. Steel became influenced by a brother of one of the persons present, and made a very striking address, with a good deal of energy and pathos. On his becoming dis-entranced and entering into the general conversation, Mary voluntarily disembodied her controlling power, and leaving the girl's form like a corpse, with the head resting against the shoulder of her friend, immediately took control of Dr. Steel, and in every possible way required proved it to be herself, she then through that manly form, turned in a jovial way and laughed at the position of the seemingly untenanted body and its limp condition, with a pleasant jest at the friend who supported it. She soon, however, returned to her own proper control and seemed to enjoy the trick she had played, in the control of the gentleman.

In a few moments she appeared peculiar, and calling the hired woman to follow her, they left the room. Soon she returned clad in an old-fashioned way, with gown, cap, cape and spectacles, etc., leaning on the arm of Charlotte as if bowed down with many years. Not one trace of the girl could be seen save in the youthful skin of the face. Taking a seat in the old arm chair, she began to talk as an old lady of olden times might be supposed to do, representing herself as the grandmother of Charlotte, giving her name, inquiring after all the relatives, old and young, asking by name for those belonging to families the girl could have known nothing about. Said she died of cancer near the right eye and temple ; called for tepid water and soft cloth, which being furnished, proceeded in the most natural manner to bathe and dress the cancer. She called for food and ate it, apparently without teeth, smoked after it, as she used to do, because her food always hurt her if she did not. She asked for knitting work. It being furnished, she found fault because the knitter did not know how to knit. Raveling, out and taking up again she knit, at the same time telling Charlotte how to knit without looking at it. She next asked for mending and other things to do.looked at the fabric of the ladies'

Angel Or Devil

dresses, asking the prices, etc., etc. She looked out at the windows, remarked how pleasant a place it was, and so continued for a full hour, never for a moment showing any sign of deception, but a veritable, honest, experienced domestic old lady. Numerous other personations might be related but this is sufficient.

When inquired of as to form materialization she said it was a truth, though she had never tried it because She did not know how, but should learn how when she found an opportunity.

During her stay at Mr. Roff's her physical condition continually improved, being under the care and treatment of her supposed parents and the advice and help of her physician. She was ever obedient to the government and rules of the family, like a careful and wise child, always keeping in the company of some of the family, unless to go into the nearest neighbors across the street. She was often invited and went with Mrs. Roff to visit the first families of the city, who soon became satisfied that the girl was not crazy, but a fine, well-mannered child.

The manner in which she acted for a considerable time after coming into Mr. Roff's family was very strange to many. Sitting down to the tea-table on one occasion, Mrs. Roff asked:

"Now, Mary, what shall I help you to ? "

She answered:

"O, nothing, I thank you, ma, I'll go to heaven for my tea."

Angel Or Devil

Suiting the action to the word, off she went into a quiet trance or to heaven as she termed it, and so remained till the family had eaten, when she returned to her normal state. Being again asked, she said she had been to tea, and the question was put:

"Mary, what do you eat, and how do you eat it?"

Her answer was :

"O ma, if I could tell, you could not understand it."

And thus for some time she only ate in that way, except a very little occasionally, to pacify the anxious family. As her system became in better condition, she ate more freely, and for many weeks toward the last she ate. drank and slept as a healthy person should.

As the time drew near for the restoration of Lurancy to her parents and home, Mary would sometimes seem to recede into the memory and manner of Lurancy for a little time, yet not enough to lose her identity or permit the manifestation of Lurancy's mind, but enough to show she was impressing her presence upon her own body.

On being asked, *"Where is Lurancy?"* she would say, *"Gone out somewhere,' or, "She is in heaven taking lessons, and I am here taking lessons too."*

On Sunday, May 19th, about half past four o'clock, P. M.,

Angel Or Devil

Mr. Roff and Mary were sitting in the parlor, Henry Vennum, Lurancy's brother, being in the sitting room, another room and hall between. Mary left control, and Lurancy took full possession of her own body. Henry was called in and she caught him around his neck, kissed and wept over him, causing all present to weep. At this juncture, Mr. Roff was called and asked Lurancy if she could stay till Henry could go and bring her mother (she had ex- pressed a desire to go and see her father and mother) She said *"No,"* but if Henry would go and bring her, she would come again and talk with her. She immediately left and Mary came again. When Mary was asked where she had been ? she replied, *"I have seen Doctor Stevens and he looks as good as ever again."*

Mrs. Vennum was brought within an hour, and on her arrival, Lurancy came into full control, when one of the most affecting scenes ever witnessed took place. Mother and daughter embraced and kissed each other, and wept until all present shed tears of sympathy ; it seemed the very gate of Heaven.

On the morning of May 21st, Mr. Roff writes as follows :

"Mary is to leave the body of Rancy today, about eleven o'clock, so she says. She is bidding neighbors and friends good-by, Rancy to return home all right to-day. Mary came from her room up stairs where she was sleeping with Lottie, at ten o'clock last night, lay down by us, hugged and kissed us, and cried because she must bid us good by, telling us to give all her pictures, marbles and cards, and twenty-five cents Mrs. Vennum had given her, to Rancy, and had us promise to visit Rancy often." She tells me to write to Dr. Stevens as follows:

"Tell him I am going to heaven, and Rancy is coming home well. She says she will see your dear children in spirit life; says she saw you on Sunday last.' * * She said last night, weeping, 'O pa, I am going to heaven to-morrow at eleven o'clock, and Rancy is coming back cured, and going home all right.' She talked most lovingly about the separation to take place, and most beautiful was her talk about heaven and her home."

Mrs. Alter writes :

"When the day came, and the angels told Mary that Lurancy was coming to take full possession of her own body, it seemed to make her feel very sad. She went to the residences of Mr. L. C. Marsh and Mr. M. Hoober, to say good-by, telling them the angels had said the body was cured, and Lurancy was coming to go home and live with her parents again all well, yet she says, 'I feel sad at parting with you all, for you have treated me so kindly ; you have helped by your sympathy to cure this body, and Rancy can come and inhabit it.'"

This shows that the angels can help the children of earth. Mr. M. Hoober being a pious Christian gentleman, and loving

Mary for her sweet influence in his family, came into the room and asked if she would like to sing with him and his good wife. She said: *"Yes, I am so sad, but when I go to heaven all tears will be wiped away, and I will be happy."*

After singing they all knelt down, and Mr. Hoober made a very affecting prayer, saying, *"If it can be that an angel is in our midst, and about to leave us to go and join her own in spirit-life, will God in his goodness allow her to bear a message of love to my own angel father and loved ones, who may, for all we can see, be hovering around our household at this moment."* He hoped we would all be better and wiser, and when Lurancy should come back to her normal condition, would be better for the strange and new lessons she has learned.

Mary had sent word to her sister Nervie to come to her father's to stay an hour with her. to say good-by, and when Rancy should come back at eleven o'clock, to take her to Mr. Roff's office, and he would go to Mr. Vennum's with her. Mary said: *"I will come in spirit as close to you as I can, and comfort you in sorrow, and you will feel me near you sometimes."*

When eleven o'clock came she seemed both to go or let Lurancy come back. Mrs. Alter started to go home and Mary started with her. When in the yard, Mrs. A. said, *"Mary, you have always done as you said you would, but as I don't understand these things, will you please let Lurancy come back just now, and then you can come again if you want to."* Mary said: *"Yes, I will,"* and she kissed mother and sister good-by.

A voice said, *"Why, Mrs. Alter, where are we going?"* Then in a breath, *"Oh, yes, I know, Mary told me "*

On the way they met Mrs. Marsh and Mrs. Hoober, who were the nearest neighbors and Mary's favorite friends; Lurancy did not seem to know them, but remarked, 'Mary thinks so much of these neighbors." Then turning to Mrs. Alter, with whom Lurancy had been but slightly acquainted two years ago, she said, *"Mrs. Alter, Mary can come and talk to you nearly all the way home, if you want her to, and then I will comeback."* She spoke, and appeared like one slightly acquainted. Mrs. Alter said *"I have trusted you in the past, and of course I would love to talk with my sister."*

The change was again made, and Mary said, *"I do love to be with you so much."*

She talked lovingly, and gave good advice about many things and family matters. The final change now took place at the time predicted, and Lurancy stated she felt something as though she had been asleep, yet she knew she had not. On reaching Mr. Roff's office, she addressed him as Mr. Roff, and asked if he would take her home, which

Angel Or Devil

he did.

May 22nd, Mr. Roff writes me as follows:

"Thank God and the good angels, the dead is alive and the lost is found. I mailed you a letter yesterday at half past ten o'cock. M., stating that Mary had told us she would go away, and Rancy return at eleven o'clock the 21st of May. Now I write you that at half past eleven o'clock A. M., Minerva called at my office with Rancy Vennum, and wanted me to take her home, which I did. She called me Mr. Roff, and talked with me as a young girl would, not being acquainted. I asked her how things appeared to her if they seemed natural. She said it seemed like a dream to her. She met her parents and brothers in a very affectionate manner, hugging and kissing each one in tears of gladness. She clasped her arms around her father's neck a long time, fairly smothering him with kisses. I saw her father just now (eleven o'clock). He says she has been perfectly natural, and seems entirely well. You see my faith in writing you yesterday morning instead of waiting till she came."

The *Watseka Republican* says:

"The meeting with her parents at the home was very affecting, and now she seems to be a healthy, happy little girl, going about noting things she saw before she was stricken, and recognizes changes that have since taken place. This is a remarkable case, and the fact that we cannot understand such things, does not do away with the existence of these unaccountable manifestations. "

The Danville Illinois Times, in speaking of this case, says :

"Mr. and Mrs. Roff are Spiritualists, and stoutly maintain that their daughter's ability to penetrate closed books and letters in the manner indicated, was imparted by the inhabitants of an unseen world. We have no fixed opinion as to whether Spiritualism is false or true. Certain it is, that occurrences are upon record which are hard to explain upon any natural hypothesis, but attributable to spirits' aid. Let those say who know, for we do not. In spite of all opposition, Spiritualists have increased in numbers, nor are they confined to the illiterate classes, but embrace poets, scholars and statesmen. Let us hope the unharmful truth will early assert a glorious reign, and illuminate the darkened understanding of men."

The Iroquois County Illinois Times, under the head of "Mesmeric Mysteries," and in reference to Lurancy Vennum, says :

"Mr. and Mrs. Roff kindly offered to take charge of her until her mind would change, and she would become well again. She went there in February, and remained till about three weeks ago. Since then she has been Lurancy Vennum, and is healthy and full of intelligence. * * It was hard for even the most skeptical not to believe there was something supernatural about her. She was not prompted by the spirit of Mary Roff, how could she know so much about the family, people with whom she was not acquainted, and whom she had never visited. * * No stranger would have suspected her of being the victim of disease, though her eyes were unusually bright. * * "There are yet numberless mysteries in this world, though science has dissipated many wonders, and philosophy has made plain many marvels. There is much that is unaccountable in the action of spiritualistic and they do many things that puzzle the greatest philosophers. Skeptical and unbelieving as we are, and slight as our experience has been, we have seen enough to convince us that Spiritualism is not all humbug. The case of Lurancy Vennum, a bright young girl of fourteen years, has been the subject of much discussion in Watseka during the past year, and there is a good deal in it beyond human comprehension. "

The subject of this article had become familiar with the writer during the several months she was under his advice and the more kindly care and sympathy of Mr. Roff's family, speaking with him freely up- on every subject necessary to her good and the courtesies of association, always, however, in the presence of members of the family. On Sunday, the second day of June, he met her with her parents at the house of a friend, who lived nearly two miles from Mr. Vennum's. Lurancy was introduced to him by Mr. Vennum. She seemed to be an entire stranger, and for two hours remained like a timid, unacquainted child. The next day, June 3rd, without notice to any one, the writer went to the house of a noted attorney, and as he entered the gate, Lurancy came out the door, stopped on the steps and said, *"How do you do, Doctor ? Mary Roff told me to come here and meet you. Somehow she makes me feel you have been a very kind friend to me ;"* and she would not let him into the house till she had delivered a long message from Mary. Since the last interview he has seen her several times, and she seems easy, affable, and as a young lady should.

On the 25th of June she wrote a beautiful letter, by the consent of her friends saying among other things:

"Dear Doctor, I am feeling quite well to-day. I was up to Mrs. Alter s to-day ; she is very well at present. This afternoon I called at Mr. Roff s office, and had quite a long talk with him ; but of course it was about the loving angels that you and I love so well. Let them twine around your neck their arms and press upon your brow their kiss. * * Well, Doctor, you have many dear friends in this city who love you much.

I saw Mrs. M----- . She said she would have died if it had not been for you, and you know about Mrs. I----- . We know you saved her life. * * Kiss your loving wife for me, and tell her we shall all meet in heaven if not on earth. I shall visit Mrs. Roff tomorrow. * * I shall have my picture taken and send it to you in mv next letter. I get up early and take the morning air. I should like to have you write a line to me.

Your friend,

                LURANCY VENNUM

This letter, written in pencil, is very different in its make-up and penmanship from those written by the same hand, signed by Mary Roff, and gives evidence of another mind. Since penning the foregoing article, the writer has received the following letter from the mother of Lurancy, through the politeness of Mr. Roff:

WATSEKA, ILL., July 9th, 1878.

DEAR FRIEND,

Mary L. Vennum is perfectly and entirely well, and perfectly natural. For two or three weeks after her return home, she seemed a little strange to what she had been before she was taken sick last summer, but only, perhaps, the natural change that had taken place with the girl, and except it seemed to her as though she had been dreaming or sleeping, etc. Lurancy has been smarter, more intelligent, more industrious, more womanly and more polite than before. We give the credit of her complete cure and restoration to her family, to Dr. E. W. Stevens and Mr. and Mrs. Roff, by their obtaining her removal to Mr. Roff's, where her cure was perfected. We firmly believe that had she remained at home, she would have died, or we would have been obliged to send her to the insane asylum, and if so, that she would have died there, and that further, that I could not have lived but a short time with the care and trouble devolving on me. Several of the relatives of Mary Lurancy, including ourselves, now believe she was cured by spirit power, and that Mary Roff controlled the girl.

MRS. LURINDA VENNUM.

On the 10th of July Mr. Roff writes:

Dear Doctor,

Mr. Vennum is out of town, but 1 have often talked with him, and I know his opinion, often expressed, that Lurancy and her mother would both have died if we had not taken the girl ; he gives all credit to yourself and us for it. He believes it was spirit agency that did the work. Lurancy is in perfect health, and "much more womanly than before" (so her mother says). She says she used to romp and play with her brothers, and with the horses, etc. Now she is steady; you can hardly imagine how the dear girl loves those who saved her. She sends you a letter to-day, but thinks it a little strange you have not answered her last letter.

Yours, etc., A. B. ROFF.

In the letter referred to above, the child writes :

I am quite well, and much obliged that you showed my

letter to your dear wife. I am sure there is nothing for me to be ashamed of. * * I was down to Mr. M's store, and he told me how you saved his wife's life, and they appreciate it. Will you want me to give you my description of heaven ? I will sometime, when there are but few present. I can't write it, for I make so many mistakes. I made a short call at Mrs. Alter's. Please ask your daughter to write to me. Can't you bring your wife when you come ? Poor Mr. Wickersham still lives. We should pity such mortals. My aunt says I know all that has transpired, but none know but the angels and you.

Your friend,
                              MARY L. VENNUM

       On the evening of the 16th of July, 1878, in the parlors of Asa B. Roff and his wife, we, the undersigned, met and listened to the careful reading and consideration of the foregoing narrative, and declare it to be entirely true and correct in every respect ; and
further, that now after eight weeks of home life, Lurancy Vennum remains well and sound in body and mind.
                              ASA B. ROFF,
                              ANN ROFF,
                              THOMAS J. VENNUM.
                              LURINDA VENNUM.

Angel Or Devil

WATSEKA, Iroquois Co., Ill.,
July 18th, 1878.

TO THE READER: The writer has collated the foregoing facts from a mass of interesting incidents, which might be much enlarged upon, but he is satisfied with the few incidents that involve principles hitherto discussed by the philosophic world, and sends them out to make a chapter in the literature of Spiritualism. He has this day seen the family, including the subject of the narrative. Mrs. Vennum has gone to Indiana for a two weeks' rest and visit, and left Lurancy in charge of the family and house, a healthy, happy, noble girl.

E. WINCHESTER STEVENS.
July 19th, 1878

MARY LURANCY VENNUM

Views of Prominent Spiritualists in Reference to the Manifestations through her Organism, as Detailed in the Foregoing Narrative. In reference to the case of angelic incarnation (Mary Roff and Lurancy Vennum) reported by Dr. Stevens, there is no reed of endorsement or comment by Scientists, on such facts so well reported. When the sun shines we need no professor of optics to teach us the fact.

Angel Or Devil

One such example of angel visitations to earth, would enlighten all the world, if it were not for the stubborn hostility to truth of the materialistic press and fossilized church, which causes the systematic suppression and concealment of such information from the people, and imposes upon all who are really enlightened the duty of aiding in the diffusion of this narrative. I think that every Spiritualist should purchase as many copies of this remarkable narrative as he can afford, and distribute them among honest inquirers.

I would add a word in reference to the marvelous fact of spirit exchange or transfer of souls between two bodies. All spiritualists are familiar with the trance mediumship in which one from the Spirit world occupies a human body while the spirit of that body is either resting quietly, or, as has happened in some cases, gone out to obsess another body. Experience shows that this is not a hazardous or unnatural thing, but it is very strange to those who have not learned the rudiments of spiritual science. By way of explanation I would say that spirit is far more easily transferred than matter, and that the exchange of souls between Mary Roff and Lurancy Vennum is no more marvelous to those who understand it than the pouring of a quart of water from a full pitcher into one just emptied.

The spiritual potency of a dose of medicine of any kind

(morphine, quinine or any other drug) held in the hands by any one who is not of a hard temperament, will pass up the arm and pervade the whole person. It may also be arrested in its progress at the arm and by a few dispersive passes thrown out of the body entirely : or it may be transferred by contact into the person of another individual, thus relieving the one who first felt it of the drug symptoms.

As the psycho-physiological effects are so easily transferred, and as pains are often transmitted from one who is suffering them to a healing operator whose touch gives relief psychic impressions are still more easily transferred. The intense melancholy or joy felt by one individual is often suddenly transferred to another even without touch, at the first approach of a sympathetic person.

But personal presence is not necessary. A letter held by a psycho-meter on the forehead will give the entire force of the emotions of the writer and a consciousness of, his whole character, which is vividly felt. Sometimes the impression is so complete that the psycho-meter becomes lost in the character, and actually personates it; as in Boston thirty-four years ago, an intellectual lady, in describing Mr. Clay under the influence of his autograph, at length lost her identity and assuming the dignity of Mr. Clay, declined to be catechized any longer as to her impressions. Mr.

Angel Or Devil

Clay was then living.

The extremely impressional or sensitive individual, may thus take on any character by merely coming into psychometric rapport with it, and for a time personate the individual, giving a very good embodiment of his character. Indeed a considerable portion of that which has been considered spiritual obsession is of this sympathetic or psychometric character, and is sometimes a tolerable expression of the spirit's sentiments, although the spirit may have nothing to do with it. The same sympathetic sort of quasi-obsession may take place concerning living individuals, and the psychometric medium may personate and speak or write for a living individual, as in the case of a girl in Ohio, who at the same sitting wrote a prescription from Dr. Hahnemann, the founder of Homeopathy and another from Dr. Hill, a living physician.

Thus a spiritual transfer of thought may take place by receptivity, when the party supposed to speak, is entirely passive. But when that party is active his psychic power and personality are transmitted far more effectively even when the recipient is not endeavoring to receive them. Dr. Brittan tells of his own success in projecting his spirit so as to be seen and recognized by persons at a distance, and Dr. Jno. F. Gray of this city, a distinguished physician, by making the effort to look into the condition of a patient whom he could not conveniently visit, made so strong an impression on the man (who was not expecting him, that he firmly insisted that Dr. Gray did visit him and stand by his bedside where he saw him) and remarked on the strangeness of the fact that Dr. Gray would come to see him and walk off without saying anything. Hundreds of such cases are reported in spiritual literature, as well as similar cases in which the party came out of himself spiritually, has like Swedenborg visited the Spirit-world and seen his friends, or has seen and described others to the satisfaction of their surviving friends.

It is quite a familiar old story for the last hundred years that clairvoyants in mesmeric somnambulism visit distant places and describe them minutely ; and the Spirit world has often been described by the somnambulists who have visited it.

There is nothing in this **"Watseka Wonder"** which is not illustrated by parallel facts and experiments, although they are but little known to the world. But in none other do we find so satisfactory an array of public and private events, combined with the peculiar angelic beauty of sentiment which is displayed and which is so honorable to all concerned. A deeply interesting volume might be made by compiling these authentic narratives.

So easy is the interchange between the two contiguous worlds, that spirits have often eaten of earthly food in their materialization, which has disappeared forever as their new bodies vanished, and, on the other hand, living women, like Mollie Fancher, of Brooklyn, have been spiritually fed while fasting for many months and been thus sustained in health like Mary Roff. "I have food which ye know not" is the language that may often be used by spiritual ecstatics.

This Watseka case is interesting as an illustration of the elevated and beautiful nature of spirit communion, and the gradual elevation of mankind by its increasing frequency and power. The "communion of saints' which orthodoxy has failed to realize is to become hereafter a grand factor in human elevation, and, as the centuries roll on, the still *accumulating* power of the Spirit-world, organized for earthly labors of love and aided by the increasing spirituality of mankind, will surround our lives with sweet influences as if we were breathing another atmosphere, and standing in the presence of all that is holy.

J. E. BUCHANAN.
No. 1 Livingston Place, New York.

Views of D. P. Kayner, M. D.

There gathers around the case given to the public through the RELIGIO - PHILO- SOPHICAL JOURNAL, under the above heading, an unusual amount of interest. Being personally well acquainted with Mr. A. B. Roff and his family, and having some acquaintance with Dr. Stevens, and knowing they are not persons who would in any manner lend themselves to a deception in this matter, it assumes increased proportions in its importance as a wonderful phenomenon in which are displayed many principles relating to the spiritual philosophy; notably among which are first, the effects of bodily disease in favoring the influence of uncongenial or undeveloped controls; secondly, he influence of cultivated and properly directed mesmeric power in changing those controls for more congenial ones; and, third, while thus healing the physical body through changing the controls, and apparently changing the individuality of the person controlled, giving a spirit, who had through a similar disease been deprived of a full earth experience, an opportunity to enter again into those earthly relations and increase her experience amid earthly surroundings. Taken all together, it is one of the best authenticated illustrations of the phenomena and philosophy of Spiritualism among the millions of phenomena which have been presented to the world, and the solution of the complex problems of the philosophy of life, embodied in the phases presented, will greatly tend to elucidate life s many mysteries.

That certain diseases, as epilepsy or catalepsy, predispose

to render the subject easy of control by undeveloped spirits, seems to have been settled by this case. The changed polarity of the brain-magnets, deranges the harmonious control of the individual spirit over its body by temporarily suspending the connection, and blending of the action of the spirit body or soul with the physical body, through which the manifestations of mind are shown. In this condition another spirit having sufficient knowledge of the psychic laws may form a connection with the external organs of the mind, either by acting directly upon the brain itself, or seizing upon the spirit body of the individual thus affected, and through that, by taking possession of the brain and its organs, hold control of the mind ; and, acting upon any of the faculties at will, sway the thoughts, words and actions of the individual, thus said to be *"obsessed"* at their pleasure.

Another important lesson derived is. that calm, cultivated and properly directed mesmeric power is capable of changing the control and, in a manner, of influencing and directing the operations of minds in the mundane and supra-mundane spheres. In this we can begin to see some of the philosophy of "the gift of healing."

The spirit who has learned the law of self-control, whose cultivated reason holds the reins and guides the intellect, who readily comprehends the necessities of the hour and grasps them with the strong grip of an educated Will, has that within him which, when properly directed, is more effective in restoring a healthy polarity to a diseased brain and correcting all mental derangement than all other means combined. And this applies with equal force to spirits in the form or those who have departed this life. The mental influences with which an invalid is surrounded and the manner in which his own mental machinery is set in motion and made to operate thereby is, when adapted to the necessities of the case, more potent than drugs in effecting a cure.

    The healing power which can be imparted and aroused through the psychic forces are multitudinous, and vast in their proportions. Disease may be said to be any derangement in the proper balancing of the working forces of body or mind, and the adjustment of those forces, restoring the equilibrium, will bring a return of health. Changing the polarity of the brain-magnets deranges the individual psychic control over the bodily functions, and can only be restored to a normal action through some external impression or control which influences the mental machinery to resume its normal relations and assert its wonted activities. This may perhaps be accomplished through the influence of drugs ; but aside from their specific action upon special organs, they are, undoubtedly, more efficient in their operation upon the mind, in some way arousing the psychic forces which wheel the unbalanced organs into harmonious relations by which the vigor of health is regained, and the physician and his remedies are applauded.

It will however be noticed in this connection that the same medicine will act differently in the hands of different physicians and will act best in his hands who imparts the most genial and positive psychic influences.

But, perhaps, the most difficult problem to solve, is involved in the question of *"obsession"* of the spirit leaving its own physical body and roaming at will while another spirit takes possession of the physical habitation of that spirit and re-enacts over again the scenes of its earth life and renews its earthly experiences. From 'analogy, and from the accumulated knowledge of clairvoyance, it seems clearly established that a spirit cannot completely sever its connections with the body and again re-habilitate itself therewith. Now, just how far all apparent obsession, is subjective psychological spirit control acting upon and directing the individual's own spirit to produce the manifestation presented , is difficult to determine. In this problem lies the great mystery of the"Watseka Wonder," and its proper solution will do more to unravel the tangled skein of the power of mind on mind, of mind over matter, and of the peculiarities of mediumship, than all the sophistical arguments of the scholastic world.

The subject of obsession has engaged the attention of some

of the ablest minds in the world. Andrew Jackson Davis from the heights of clairvoyance, if we rightly understand him, considers it an utter impossibility for one's spirit to leave his body or be displaced by another spirit. While on the contrary, a case so clearly verified as the one under consideration will have more weight in deciding this question than all mere theories and assertions.

Again what are we to do with the case, where on a vessel wrecked at sea, one of the famishing persons on the wreck became unconscious and lay almost as one dead for two hours? On awakening he informed the captain a vessel was steering to their relief. During the time he was lying in the unconscious state upon the wreck, he was seen by the mate of the relieving vessel to enter the Captain's state room and write upon his slate, *"Steer due North- west,"* and after the rescue, when pointed out to the captain as the mysterious person who had done the writing, on being asked to write the above sentence on the opposite side of the slate, the correspondence was perfect.

The case of a medium in Connecticut hunting up a sea captain for the captain's wife, finding and conversing with him in London, giving him his wife's message, and being seen by the captain sufficiently to be recognized by him on his return, while the medium's body, in an apparently dead state, was lying in the shade of an apple tree, is worthy of consideration.

Angel Or Devil

To what sublime heights may not man soar, if he possesses the power to step out of his mortal tenement at will, through a knowledge and application of psychic law, and leaving the body in charge of some other spirit, enters upon the experience of the life beyond to return and re-inhabit the body again at the pleasure of the two spirits thus exchanging experiences? Which, of the two propositions involved in this question is the true one, calls for our most devoted endeavors to discover. Taken all in all this "Watseka Wonder" being so well verified, forms one of the most interesting and important chapters in the history of Spiritualism.

Letter From Dr. S. B. Brittan.

To THE EDITOR of THE RELIOIO-PHILOSOPHIOAL JOURNAL:

I have read the narrative of E. "W. Stevens, published in late numbers of the JOURNAL. The alleged facts are certainly extraordinary, but they are compassed by spiritual forces, and compatible with the psycho-physiological laws. The internal evidence that the statement accords with the essential facts of the case, is such as to secure a general acceptance of the Doctor's testimony among those who may have been familiar with similar phenomena, and all who are able to comprehend the philosophy of their causation. In the attempt to obtain credence for marvelous statements which have no foundation in either fact, law or reason, the narrator is almost sure to blunder by the introduction of some alleged occurrence which involves an impossibility. The man who knows little or nothing of the essential forces and fundamental laws which govern spiritual phenomena, has no certain means of determining what is, and what is not, within the range of possibilities. A single illustration will serve to elucidate my idea.

Many years ago, while the writer was editing the *Spiritual Telegraph,* a tricky fellow sent us a long account of remarkable facts, said to have occurred at West Troy. In his story of the wonders alleged to have been performed by spiritual agency, he declared that a table rose from the floor without hands ; that it floated out-of one open window, 'and after remaining suspended, mid air, over the sidewalk for a little time, it slowly returned through another open window and resumed its former position. Had the narrator stopped at this point in his story, we could only have said, well, the alleged facts are remarkable, but they are altogether possible; and then our acceptance or rejection of the statement would have been determined by our judgment of the credibility of the witness. Instead of pausing, however, in time to prevent an impeachment of his veracity, he went on to say that he measured both the table and the window, and found that the former was fifteen inches wider the narrowest way than the latter. In other words, this Munchhausen story-teller made an inflexible object one utterly incapable of the slightest compressibility pass through a space between unyielding walls, fifteen inches less than it was known to occupy, and without breaking either the frame or fiber of the table. It required but little philosophy to decide that such an assumed fact, if not altogether impossible, in the nature of things, was at least highly improbable.

The same party sent us some half dozen similar communications, every one in a new chirography, and mailed at a different post office. But we spotted the author every time; marked his papers *"bogus,"* and thrust them all into the same pigeon-hole. Sometime after the writer received a brief note from this pretended medium, dated and postmarked at Brooklyn. The material portions of the note were as follows :

SIR: I perceive that you are an old bird, and not to be taken on chaff.

I thought I could sell you out, but you are too d------d sharp for me."

Subsequently this same miserable trickster ventured on a further trial of his experiment by sending his villainous inventions to the late Hon. Horace Greeley, whose motto adopted with special and exclusive reference to this subject was, "Give us the facts; we want no philosophy." The editor of the *Tribune* published the statements, with an implied editorial endorsement, when a little philosophy would have enabled him to detect the fraud and expose the impostor.

My own investigation of the facts and laws of mind and matter, as displayed in the relations of spirits to the phenomena of psycho-physiology, assures me that there is nothing in the narrative of Dr. Stevens that is intrinsically incredible ; and in all such cases we have only to satisfy ourselves, and, if possible, the public, of the intelligence, discrimination and veracity of the witnesses. It is quite natural for the average physician, who is usually a man of small faith and a materialist in his philosophy, to refer all such spiritual phenomena to physical causes. The familiar diagnosis resolves all spasmodic attacks, such as the Doctor has described, into epilepsy, catalepsy and hysteria. It is safe to assume that these conditions and various forms of disease may, and often do, result from the operation of both physical and spiritual causes. They may be produced by any violent disturbance of the subtile forces on which the vital functions and voluntary motion are made to depend. The abnormal action of the individual's own mind, and the violence of his passions ; the presence and influence of powerful magnetic forces emanating from other persons, whose minds and lives are disorderly ; and the direct agency of spirits of another world, whose unfinished or otherwise unsatisfactory lives prompt them to come back in the hope of recovering what was lost, and performing what was left undone, are chief among the causes and influences which derange the human body and mind. The spirits of the class referred to exist in great numbers along the borderline between the two worlds, and it is not strange that they raid across the frontiers of our visible existence, in some cases to our injury.

It may assist the reader to form an intelligent judgment of the facts comprehended in the narrative of your correspondent, if I briefly analyze the peculiar forms of disease to which such phenomena are usually referred. Epilepsia, or epilepsy, is otherwise known in common parlance as "the falling sickness." The word is derived from the Greek, and literally signifies to seize upon. The application of the classical word appears to have been determined by the suddenness of the attack ; and the propriety of the familiar terms employed to represent the disease, must be evident to any one who has ever witnessed the sudden manner in which the patient falls to the ground in an epileptic fit. The ancients regarded this as "the sacred disease," for the reason that it disordered the mind the noblest part of our human nature and also because they attributed its existence to spiritual causes.

The victim of this fearful malady sometimes has little or no warning of the attack ; but in other cases, and more frequently, the paroxysm is preceded by certain symptoms, some of which are cognizable by the patient and the qualified observer. The symptom most frequent in the experience of the subject, is a feeling of coldness, as if occasioned by a light current of air proceeding from some part of the body, usually the lower portion of the spinal column, or from the region of the kidneys. This peculiar feeling is known to the faculty as the aura epileptic. Other symptoms are diminished contractile power of the muscles, a feeling of debility, flatulence, palpitation and stupor. As the cool, creeping sensation approaches the head, the subject becomes dizzy ; sensation, consciousness and voluntary motion are suspended; the paroxysm follows, and may last from one minute to a quarter of an hour or longer, during which the muscles are powerfully convulsed, the respiration difficult, the patient froths at the mouth, the features are distorted and the face flushed or otherwise discolored. The attack is followed by a feeling of unusual lassitude and a disposition to sleep.

    This disease no doubt results from a great variety of physical causes and incidental conditions occurring in the experience of the individual. Among these I may mention organic defects and hereditary predisposition ; want of a proper cerebral balance and a uniform distribution of the vital motive power ; sudden fright, heavy blows and violent shocks to the nervous system ; the change that occurs at the age of puberty and solitary vice. That it may also result from more subtile and psychological causes, and the visitations of disorderly spirits, I am equally well assured. The most enlightened of the ancient nations entertained this idea, and were disposed to ascribe all similar diseases to the invisible sphere of spiritual causation. This is sufficiently evident from the evangelical narratives of similar cases, in which all the more important phenomena of epilepsy are plainly described.

Before referring to several ancient examples, I will briefly define the nature of cataleptics, or catalepsy. In this disease sensation and all the voluntary faculties and functions of mind and body, are suddenly arrested. The organs of involuntary motion usually continue their functions; the heart and lungs moving in ordinary cases, the former with an accelerated action and diminished power. It is also characterized by unusual rigidity of the muscles. The body and limbs, though stiff and statue- like, may be moved by the effort of another, and they retain the posture in which they are left, however unnatural and uneasy the position. The particular expression on the face, at the moment of the attack, is liable to remain. The paroxysm varies in the degrees of intensity in different patients ; and the time that may transpire before the restoration to the normal condition is altogether uncertain. In profound states of catalepsy all outward signs of life sometimes disappear; the processes of the animal chemistry cease, and the trance may continue for weeks. In this state of suspended animation many persons have been buried alive, or before the spirit had severed its connection with the body.

I have neither the time nor space to attempt an exhaustive treatment of the subject, much as society needs a complete philosophy of its material facts and essential laws. My exposition of the causes and aspects of these forms of disease, must be general. I do not propose a critical classification of the symptomatic phenomena, whether physical or psychological; nor is it my purpose to consider the means and methods to be employed in the treatment of the same. It is rather my present design to call attention to a profound but much neglected subject, which, however, most deeply concerns the public welfare. Beyond this, I desire to show that the abnormal conditions and startling phenomena under consideration, may and do result from causes resident in both the material and spiritual worlds. Even when an attack of either epilepsy or catalepsy is precipitated by purely organic conditions and physical causes, the subsequent state and its phenomenal aspects are very likely to be complicated by the play of psychological forces and the interposition of spiritual visitors.

It is natural that the spirits whose lives on earth were cut short by either acts of violence or the supervention of disease, should have a desire to continue the career that terminated

Angel Or Devil

prematurely. In like manner, all who are conscious of having neglected their opportunities in this world, must desire to finish up the incomplete work of this rudimental life. Those who have committed great wrongs on earth may be forced back by a law of the moral constitution or f rom an irresistible impulse to undo the mischief of their hands to the scenes of the ruin they have made. Such spirits reviewing the records of their lives, imperishable forever in the memory earnestly seeking relief from ignorance and unhappiness, may seize on any poor, helpless mortal in the hope of deriving some satisfaction from a temporary renewal of the former relations. Filled with recollections of time wasted ; a life madly sacrificed, or at best disorderly and profitless, they are liable to derange the body and mind of any delicate subject who may willingly or otherwise yield to their influence. In all this we are not, as a rule, authorized to infer that the spirits are maliciously disposed. It may suffice that they are ignorant and clumsy to account for the disorderly results of their influence. Should a common tinker attempt to manipulate a fine chronometer, he would be sure to derange its action. The man who has never handled anything more delicate than chain cables, could never tune my lady's harp. An ignorant magnetizer, with strong passions, an unsuitable temperament and unbalanced brain, might derange and upset the nervous system of a sensitive girl, and so may an ignorant spirit, who has not yet recovered from the similar imperfections of the life on earth.

The careful reader of the New Testament will have observed, not only that cases of vital and mental derangement corresponding in all their essential features to the foregoing analyses of epilepsy and catalepsy were of frequent occurrence ; but also, that they were invariably ascribed to the agency of demons or spirits. Among the Greeks a demon was not always regarded as an evil spirit. The word was not understood to either express or imply anything in respect to his moral qualities. The ancients believed in both good and evil demons or spirits of men. When, therefore, we translate the word into English, and call the demon of the Greek Scriptures a devil, we neither change his nature nor acquire a right to defame his character. We can not make a good spirit evil by giving him a bad name. Those only who produced unhappy effects were characterized as "unclean spirits ;" by which we may understand spirits wanting intelligence and a high moral purpose. It was an important part of the business of the early Evangelical teachers, under the apostolic commission, to cast out the spirits whose influence was found to be detrimental.

The fact can not be disputed, that the different classes of demons referred to by the early Greeks embraced "the disembodied spirits of the dead, without respect to their moral qualities," and they appear to have been "the favorite -sources of information." The distinction between two general classes is clearly made in the following passage by a learned author:

"There is also a second class of demons, namely: the souls of those who having lived meritoriously have departed from the body. Such a soul I find called in the ancient Latin tongue Lemur. Of these Lemures, he, who having obtained by lot he guardianship of his posterity, presides over the house with a quiet and placable superintendence, is called the household Lar. But those, who, on account of a vicious life, having obtained no happy seats, are a sort of vagabonds, or are punished by a kind of exile ; and who inflicts idle terrors upon good men, but more real evils upon the wicked. This kind is commonly called Larvae." Apocatastasis, p. 89.

The narratives of the Evangelists contain many references to the agency of spirits, in the transfiguration of mortals, and in modifying human feeling, thought and conduct. For the time being, and as long as the spirit maintained the ascendancy over the medium, the former often governed the volition and action of the latter. As I am treating the subject in its relation to certain forms of disease, I shall make my citations from the Christian Scriptures with a special view to the illustration of that relation, and the power of Spirits to damage the organic action of mind and body. I will here introduce examples which will exhibit their demeanor and show the manner in which they handled their subjects. It is

Angel Or Devil

related that while Jesus was teaching in a synagogue in Capernaum, that there was a man present who had "an unclean spirit." The medium while under this influence was inclined to be noisy. He discovered the name and character of the Teacher, and in a declamatory style insisted on being let alone.

"And Jesus rebuked him, saying, 'Hold thy peace and come out of him.' And when the un- clean spirit had torn him, and cried out in a loud voice, he came out of him." (Mark, chap. I, 35-26.)

When Jesus was coming out of a ship in which he had just crossed the sea of Galilee:

"Immediately there met him out of the tombs a man with an unclean spirit, who had his dwelling among the tombs; and no man could bind him, no, not with chains. He had been often bound with fetters and chains, and the chains had been plucked asunder by him, and the fetters broken in pieces: neither could any man tame him. And always, night and day, he was in the mountains, and in the tombs, crying and cutting himself with stones."

This spirit was rather boisterous in his recognition of the man who was about to exorcise him. While the man was under the influence of this spirit, Jesus asked for his name, where upon the spirit "answered, saying, 'My name is Legion; for we are many.' " (Mark, Chap. v. 2-9.)

It is recorded that as Jesus descended from the mountain, after his transfiguration, a man brought his only child to him,

Angel Or Devil

whose case is thus described:

"And, lo a spirit taketh him, and he suddenly crieth out; and it teareth him that he foameth again; and bruising him, hardly departeth from him. And as he was yet coming the devil threw him down, and tore him. And Jesus rebuked the unclean spirit, and healed the child."
(Luke, chap. IX, 38-41.)

The following is a very accurate description of the general phenomena which accompany an attack of the disease known as Epilepsy :

"And one of the multitude said, 'Master, I have brought unto thee my son, which hath a dumb spirit; and wheresoever he taketh him he teareth him, and he foameth, and gnasheth with his teeth, and pineth away'.... And when he saw him, straightway the spirit tore him; and he fell to the ground and wallowed, foaming 'And oft-times it hath cast him into the fire, and into the waters to destroy him' Jesus rebuked the foul spirit, saying unto him, 'Dumb and deaf spirit, I charge thee come out of him, and enter no more into him.' And the spirit cried and rent him sore, and came out of him: and he was as one dead; insomuch that many said, 'He is dead!'" *(Mark, chap. IX, 17-26.)*

It would seem from this description that the paroxysm was followed by a state of suspended animation. It is to be observed that this is not usually the case in epilepsy. The convulsion is followed by great general prostration clearly enough indicated in the Evangelical description by the words, *"and pineth away."* In all ordinary cases the respiratory movement continues and the process of the aeration of the blood goes on with only partial interruption. During the continuance of the paroxysm, as a rule, the respiration is heavy and difficult, while the heart's action is quick and strong, but never rhythmical; the systole and diastole occurring at irregular intervals.

It seems that Mary Roff was subject to spasmodic attacks from early infancy, whether originally produced by physical causes or spiritual agency, is quite uncertain. The general description given does not warrant the expression of a decisive opinion on this point. There appear, however, to have been indications of spiritual interference in her later experience. Her melancholy periods ; the "mania for bleeding herself; her inability to recognize her friends, and indisposition to heed the presence of other persons; her lucid intervals, in which she became highly clairvoyant; the preternatural strength developed in her delirium requiring the aid of so many persons to restrain her and the manner of her death are facts which may have depended largely on the presence and agency of Spirits. In such a case the ordinary professional treatment for epileptic or cataleptic fits, would have been powerless to afford relief; while the attempt to drown out the spirits, by flooding the house they had moved into, was if possible still more preposterous.

The case of Mary Lurancy Vennum is less obscure in its

origin. It was clearly a case of spiritual entrancement in the beginning. Had the Rev. B. M. Baker understood the nature of his commission as a preacher of the Gospel, and possessed the requisite qualifications for his office, he would never have thought of sending the girl to a lunatic asylum. Some one has said, "Satan loves to fish in troubled waters." If this is true, the atmosphere of madness, in and about an insane asylum, would furnish just the place and the occasion for disorderly spirits to assemble, and in which we might expect the patient to suffer most from their influence. I should as soon think of ordering a file and saw as a sedative for a nervous woman; or of prescribing a small room and a large brass-band as a soporific for babies.

If we accept the testimony of Dr. Stevens and the other witnesses, the record of the three months and ten days residence of Mary Roff in the body of Mary L. Vennum : forms a curious and most significant chapter in the history of Modern Spiritualism. The sweet spirit of the gentle and loving Mary; the strong proofs of her identity; how she occupied her time while a tenant at will in the mortal tabernacle of another, and the possible supra-mundane experiences of the released spirit of Lurancy; these are all matters of singular interest which invite comment; but the unexpected length of this letter admonishes me to leave the further consideration of the subject to yourself and your readers.

Angel Or Devil

You will, however, indulge me in a few concluding observations, which are not intended to be so general as in no case to admit of a special application. The poor victims of physical disease and spiritual infestation have little chance to recover their equilibrium when the professional classes, to which the interests of soul and body are intrusted, know so little of the real evils they attempt to combat. The doctors of medicine, as a rule, can not distinguish epilepsy, catalepsy, hysteria and nightmare from the shades of departed saints and sinners, who return whether for mischief or *"On errands of supernal grace"* to confirm the common faith in immortality. Cases have come under my observation in which the diagnosis of the family physician converted a vision of the Spiritual Heavens into a fit of hysteria. The mental darkness of lunacy and the light from another world are made to differ in terms, but are presumed to be about the same thing in fact. Our doctors of divinity can not perceive the difference between aberration and inspiration. In their judgment a man has no business to be inspired in these degenerate days ; and if he is, they are sure the devil is in him. The moral philosophy of Spiritualism suggests that through the medium of his own faculties and passions every man must look at whatever is external to himself. While many members of the profession are playing the devil in the sheep-fold as we learn from the papers and the courts a legitimate branch of their appropriate business "casting out devils" is entirely suspended. The clergy did not succeed in this part of the apostolic work. The concern was so run down, and the proprietors so destitute of assets that without the slightest consideration that branch of the business was transferred to the Spiritualists. If a spiritual wolf finds his way into the fold, the shepherd permits him to remain to frighten and worry the lambs ; or, perhaps, he advises sending the little innocents to bedlam for safety !

Nothing can more clearly illustrate the materialistic tendencies of many people than their disposition to ascribe all spiritual phenomena, manifested through the human organization, to a diseased condition and action of the faculties. All persons who have been visited by the angels, or otherwise rendered susceptible of spiritual influence, for nearly eighteen centuries, are confidently presumed to have been sick at the time. But why not refer the remarkable experiences of the Apostles themselves to the same source. They were men, subject to every form of physical disease, and had time to analyze their cases it would appear that they were very much like others in all their essential features. Saul certainly and the "falling sickness," while on his way to Damascus. He had been in a bad frame of mind for some time, and doubtless was bilious. He declared that he saw a great light and heard a voice. It might have been subjective thunder and lightening, occasioned by a derangement of the electrical polarities of his brain. And suddenly "he fell to the earth." The attack so deranged his nervous forces that for three days he saw nothing, and had no appetite. Ananias, a respectable citizen of Damascus, was impressed to come in and magnetize him, and his vision was speedily restored. The falling sickness proved to be a good thing in this case. It took the devil out of the man, and the patient was improved in body, mind and character. (Acts, chap. IX.)

"When Peter was in Joppa, at the house of one "Simon a tanner," he improved the occasion by going *"upon the house-top to pray,"* and there he had a sudden spasmodic attack which doubtless presented many of the aspects of catalepsy. He thought he "s&w heaven opened," and a great vessel resembling an immeasurable "sheet let down to the earth," containing in its enormous folds, the major part of the animal kingdom, (Acts x, 9-12.) When a man of poetic temperament and many womanly qualities was in Patmos, one of the Grecian Islands, he one day fell into something like a cataleptic 1 ranee. To his great astonishment the New Jerusalem, in all the glory of a divine personality like "a bride adorned for her husband" came after John, and his soul was entranced while the grand visions of the Apocalypse moved before him in stately procession.

It is the favorite hypothesis of many doctors, whose

wisdom is chiefly conspicuous in their diplomas, that all spiritual phenomena, so-called, are the results of some physical disorder. To what fathomless depths of apostasy to what gross and infidel issues is the unbelieving world tending, when its learned men (?) include the shades of the departed and the physical maladies of the living in the same category.

"Angels and ministers of grace defend us" from the titled ignorance and licensed stupidity which can not distinguish a vision of heaven from an attack of epilepsy, hysteria or the nightmare. Let the clergy anoint their eyes with finer clay and wash in the spiritual Siloam, and they will see something beyond the creed and the salary. This vulgar and profane idea, that all psychical experiences are but the offspring of disease, presumes that the perfection of the individual, and his accord with Nature, are best realized when he is most insensible of all impressions from super-terrestrial sources.

This monstrous assumption is born of ignorance and sensuality ; it is fostered by popular science, and dry-nursed by the old theologies ; while the doctors of divinity and medicine labor to obscure the inward senses by "the foolishness of preaching" and a species of medical exorcism.

Hoping that the time may come quickly, when the passion for new sensations among our people, will give way to a growing desire for accurate knowledge,

I remain yours fraternally,

S. B. BRITTAN, M. D.

THE VIEWS OF HUDSON TUTTLE

Taking for granted the truthfulness of the persons interested, of which there appears to be no doubt, the Watseka narrative is not only among the most wonderful but is replete with interest to the student of spiritual science. It pours a flood of light on some of the most obscure questions relating to the sensibility of the spirit and its relations to the body. "We do not understand it as supporting the theory of the displacement of the spirit of the patient by that of another, but the subjection of the spirit to the will of another, as in a trance produced by magnetism in this state the spirit is passive and at rest, and the physical body has opportunity to restore its wasted energies, and further, the intimate contact of the pure spirit, would react on the body and thus hasten its restoration to health.

This is illustrated in our daily lives by sleep, which is a lower state of rest, in which the spirit reposes and leaves the physical processes of restoration to go on without waste of energy, and it is claimed by eminent authorities that this is so much more rapid during sleep than in waking hours, thai really the former is the only time that it occurs. It is also illustrated by the magnetic state of trance, which restores by resting the spirit, and reaction of another spirit on the physical body of the subject.

This opens the vast field of investigation the relation of the Spirit-world to the physical, wherein the true laws of health and disease remain to be discovered.

The return of Mary Roff to her earth life at first presents some difficulties, for had she advanced in her new life, as we suppose she should, she would have been more matured. The drift of facts recorded show that when the spirit comes in close contact with earth through a medium, it takes on more or less of the traits and stains of its former earth-life. The disease which produced its severance from the body, and the peculiarities of its character, are revived, in this case, Mary Roff, as a mature spirit, would not have been recognized by her parents; but as a child-like daughter she filled their hearts with joy. If she came at all n a satisfactory manner, she must come in the form she presented herself, and this was the easier for her to do, because of the tendency of the returning spirit to take on ts previous earthly character on contact with earthly scenes through the medium. he cause of this need not here be explained, for the fact is sufficient.

Altogether the narrative is of exceeding value, teaching us how readily our spirit friends can come to us when the way is opened, and with what eagerness they avail themselves of an opportunity. It also shadows the great power of the spirit over the body, and of the Spirit- world, when it comes in contact with us.

HUDSON TUTTLE.

Supplementary Statement by Mr. Asa B. Roff.
To THE EDITOR OF THE JOURNAL:

Being almost daily in receipt of letters from readers of the JOURNAL, inquiring as the truthfulness of the narrative entitled, The Watseka Wonder," and not having time to fully answer all their questions, I am impelled to collect from them the prominent points of inquiry and objection, and briefly reply through the JOURNAL. Persons hereafter writing me, who do not receive an answer to their letters, will seek for the information desired in this article.

One writer inquires: "*Is it a fact? or is it a story made up to see how cunning a tale one can tell?*" Another asks: "*Can the truthfulness of the narrative be substantiated outside of yourself and those immediately interested? Can it be shown that there was no collusion between the parties, and no former acquaintance?*" A reader of the JOURNAL suggests : "It is a pretty big yarn, and there might be some arrangement between the parties, or they themselves deceived." Another after saying he has read the narrative, remarks: "I confess that I am not of your faith, and I am very doubtful whether newspapers are always embodiments of sacred truths, and I wish that under your hand, as a gentlemen, you might confirm to me and other doubting friends, the strange, mysterious, and to me, fanciful, statements in those two papers. I write wholly to overcome a doubting feeling that exists with myself and friends in regard to that remarkable and wonderful personation." A lady writes: "Is the account true in every particular? I hope there is a life beyond this, but I have never had any proof."

    I furnished Dr. Stevens with all the material facts in the case, except such as were within his own knowledge. The history of the Vennum family (and Lurancy's condition up to the time he and I went to see her June 31st), I obtained from the members thereof, and the neighbors intimately acquainted with them. The narrative, as written by Dr. Stevens, is substantially true in every part and particular, yet the half has not been told, and never can be; it is impossible for pen to describe or language portray the wonderful events that transpired during that memorable fourteen weeks that the girl was at our house. The material facts of the case can be substantiated by disinterested witnesses, whose veracity cannot be questioned, and whose evidence would settle any case in a court of law. I refer you to Robert Doyle, Chas. Sherman, S. R. Hawks, Lile Marsh, J. M. Hoober, and their wives, and to Mrs. Mary Wagner, formerly Mary Lord, all residents of Watseka.

Angel Or Devil

As to "collusion," "arrangement," or "ourselves being deceived," that is simply impossible, as you will see if you carefully read the whole narrative over again. I, too, doubt whether newspapers are always "embodiments of sacred truths," but in this case I assure the writer, the *JOURNAL* does embody a very sacred truth, that of man's immortality.

The lady writes me: "I hope there is a life beyond this, but I never have had the proof. To her I would say "Carefully read and study that narrative; in that you have the proof, for surely it is contained there. That there is a life beyond this, or rather that there is no death, you may rest assured ; there is only a change simply a removal of the real man or woman from this temporary house of clay, to that house not made with hands."

"There is no death.
The stars go down to rise upon some fairer shore,
And bright in heaven's jeweled crown
They shine forevermore."

"There is no death! The leaves may fall,
The flowers may fade and pass away,
They only wait through wintry hours
The coming of the May."

Angel Or Devil

"And ever near us though unseen,
The dear immortal spirits tread,
For all the boundless Universe
Is life! there are no dead!"

Talking with Mary, we sometimes spoke of her death. She would quickly reply : *"I never died,"* or *"I did not die."* She never tired of talking of the life beyond this. She would at any time leave her play, her reading or her jovial companions, to talk with her *"pa" and "ma"* about heaven and the angels, as she termed spirit-life, and spirits that have left the body.

I have questioned Lurancy Vennum on different occasions, as to whether she remembered anything that occurred during the time that Mary had control of her organism, and she states that a very few things occurring the last month that she was controlled, she recollects, but that in all cases the information was imparted by Mary.

In conclusion, let me say to those who doubt or disbelieve the *"strange, mysterious and wonderful story,"* call to mind Lurancy's condition at her home last January, surrounded with all the kind care of parents, friends and physicians, every thing done to alleviate her suffering and perform a cure that human minds and hands could possibly do, yet growing continually worse (if that were possible), given up by her physicians, her friends without a

Angel Or Devil

ray of hope, the insane asylum ready to receive her, a condition terrible to behold! Then view her condition from May 21st until to-day, over three months, a bright, beautiful, happy, healthy girl, and then tell me what produced the change. The narrative furnishes the facts ; account for them if you can, on any other hypothesis, than power exercised through or by the spirit of Mary Roff having control of Lurancy's body.

I am now 60 years old ; have resided in Iroquois county thirty years, and would not now sacrifice what reputation I may have by being a party to the publication of such a narrative, if it was not perfectly true. If any should desire testimonials of my standing, Col Bundy has some to use as he deems best.

Watseka, Ill., Aug. 23rd, 1878.

Asa B. Roff.

The name of this gentleman has lately be- come of much interest to our readers in connection with the case of Lurancy Vennum. From a somewhat lengthy biographical sketch of Mr. Roff, published last January in the *Iroquois County Times,* a paper printed at Watseka, we make the following extracts : 'a gentleman now in his 60th year, though with a heart as young and happy as that of a child ; agreeable, generous and full of sympathy, he is respected by all who know him, while his more intimate friends love and honor him for his personal worth.' His present enviable standing among his fellow-men is entirely owing to his indomitable energy and integrity of purpose. His family is a most exemplary one; all who know them love them; no family in our community are more happy in their domestic relations. May it ever be so with them. The above extracts in connection with the following letters, would seem to establish Mr. Rolf's reputation for truth and veracity beyond all question: WATSEKA, ILL., Aug. 22, 1878. Editor Religio -Philosophical Journal.

Dear Sir,

Many inquiries are made of me as to the standing of Mr. Asa B. Roff. These questions are .elicited through the publication in your journal of Dr. E. W. Stevens' account of the Mary Roff and Lurancy Vennum phenomena. 1 wish to say to you that no man in this community stands higher in the estimation of the people than Mr. Roff. He is a high-minded, honorable gentleman who would spurn to give currency to any thing not verified by facts. I don't believe Mr. Roff capable of a mean act. It is not in his nature.
Very truly yours,   MATTHEW H. PETERS,
         Mayor of Watseka and Editor Iroquois Times.

I have been personally acquainted with Asa B. Roff since the year 1858, and take pleasure in stating that his character and reputation

Angel Or Devil

for truth and veracity is good. CHAS. H. WOOD,

Ex-Judge 20th Circuit of Illinois.

122 LaSalle st, Chicago, Aug. 22, 1878.

We have also received letters speaking in the highest terms of Mr .Roff and family, from the following gentlemen of Watseka: O. F. McNeill, Ex-County Judge; O. C. Munhall, Postmaster ; Eobert Doyle, Attorney at Law ; John W. Eiggs, Circuit Clerk ; Henry Butzow, County Clerk ; Thomas Vennum, former Circuit Clerk; Franklin Blades, Judge of the Eleventh Judicial Circuit; M. B. Wright, County Judge.

THE END

Angel Or Devil

WATCH THE MOVIE

featuring

THE WATSEKA WONDER STORY

THE POSSESSED

a BOOTH BROTHERS documentary

www.thepossessedmovie.com

Angel Or Devil

INTRODUCTION

THE STRANGE CASE OF THE POSSESSED

"She was a normal child. A normal teenager. What she went through can only be classified as a possession. Kelly would stand and stare, in the middle of the night, at her parents. It was obvious by the look in her eyes, that the thoughts she was having, was to kill her family."

"I kept getting this feeling like I was worthless, that there was nothing left for me to do but to just kill myself," Kelly said.

She began cutting herself. Cuts that were meant to relieve any sort of pain that she was going through. Cuts that if she harmed herself she wouldn't have to harm her parents. Kelly tried cutting her arms and taking lots of pills. She explains:

"I cut pretty deep. It got so bad it started scarring up my arms. I tried covering them up so no one would see them. Sometimes it was just to cut it, release it and let it out. Then sometimes it was, do it deeper, do it harder. I just started getting really mean and I didn't like nobody. I just wanted to stay in my room and listen to music. I kept wanting to stab them and hurt them really bad and watch them bleed. It was horrible."

"Possession is very common with children. When they are inflicted, you never know what is actually going to come through them. *You never know if it's going to be something on a negative level or if it's going to be something on a positive,"* explained John Zaffis.

Dewi Morgaine a young girl from Germany found herself waking up in bed covered in blood. She felt a connection to this story and in her broken English she agreed to talk to us.

"I don't even remember what exactly happened. I just know there was a razor lying beside my bed. I woke up and I saw blood everywhere, on my arms and on the sheets. I cut myself with razor blades, with glass, anything that was sharp enough to make myself bleed. It was like someone or something dark was inside of me."

"My mother cried when I bled and I would laugh very mean at her. It felt healthy to cut. I became obsessed with seeing my own blood. If I saw my own blood it felt satisfying. Something in me screamed that I shouldn't do it. My father came to me and said, "Dewi, those are not your eyes..... Those eyes are the devil's eyes."

Dewi now in tears, feeling broken she tells us of how it began:

"I was possessed when I was thirteen years old. It took a long time and it was difficult for me to breathe. I was like 'Why I can't breathe?' I had it very much of the time. My parents brought

me to a medium. A very good psychic. She asked me if I had problems with breathing. 'I do, I said, actually I have a lot of problems with breathing. She then told me that it is because... It's because you have a demon hanging around your neck.'"

The story of Marcus's possession entailed an investigation in the local graveyard. As we interviewed both the Mother Anita and her son Marcus, it was clear that she would have done anything to save her son including taking on the demon herself. Marcus recalls,

"I was growling, saying things that I normally wouldn't say. You know, I was trying to be physical with people. I got this really cold feeling all over my body and I just went blank. When I came to, I had three to four bounty hunters and police holding on to me."

His Mother Anita describes that crazy night.

"Marcus fell down, his arms went limp and he started shaking. He was foaming at the mouth and his eyes was dilated back in his head. So I immediately thought he was having a convulsion. But when I touched him I could feel an energy, it was like electricity coming from him."

"Get off of my son now, I screamed!" Come into me you bastard, come into me!" Marcus's eyes were now glowing,

reddish looking as his facial features were trying to change on me. He was cussing, he lunged at me. He was literally trying to hurt me and the police was all on him trying to hold him back."

Anita continued with her fight, *"Come out of him, I command you! As I walk through the valley of death, I shall fear no evil. Come into me, I command you. Now look at me, look at me. I fear you not."*

Anita and Marcus had worked with us on several paranormal investigations. The video footage of Marcus's possession is mind blowing but it is nothing compared to a Mother's battle to save her son.

The one most common similarity that stood out of all these cases of possession was a memory that all the victims remembered. They all had heard rhythmic sounds of marching feet of soldiers, drums and scratching sounds. I had read this type of description in my previous research but where? Then it dawned on me, I had read this in the real Exorcist's diary. I had been given a copy of this diary 'more like a journal' from a forensic psychiatrist and doctor of neuroscience for my studies of possession. There were only six copies known to be made with the original in the safety of the Vatican.

Below is an excerpt from the real Exorcist diary written in 1949 by Rev. Raymond Bishop. The possessed boys name is

Angel Or Devil

represented by the letter R.

January 15, 1949, at the home of R in Cottage City, Maryland a dripping noise was heard by R and his Grandmother in the Grandmother's bedroom. This noise continued for a short time and then the picture of Christ on the wall shook as if the back of the wall had been thumped. By the time the parents of R returned home there was a very definite scratching sound under the floor boards near the grandmother's bed. From this night on, the scratching, was heard every night about seven o'clock and would continue until midnight. The family thought that the scratching was caused by a rodent of some kind. An exterminator was called in who placed chemicals under the floor boards, but the scratching sound continued and became more distinct when people stamped on the floor.

This scratching continued for ten days and then stopped. The family finally believed that the rodent had died. The boy, R seemed to think he still heard the noise but the family did not hear anything for a period of three days. When the sound became audible again, it was no longer in the upstairs bedroom but had moved downstairs to the boy's bedroom. It was heard as the sound of squeaking shoes along the bed and was heard only at night when the boy went to bed. The squeaking sound continued for six nights, and on the sixth night scratching again was audible.

Angel Or Devil

The mother, grandmother and boy while lying on the bed on this night heard something coming toward them similar to the rhythm marching feet and the beat of drums. The sound would travel the length of the mattress and then back and repeat this action until the mother asked "Is this you, Auntie?" (The Aunt had died in St. Louis two weeks after the first sounds were heard in the home of R). The mother continued asking questions but had no verbal reply. She asked this question, "If you are R's Auntie, knock three times." There were waves of air striking the grandmother, mother and the boy, and three distinct knocks were heard on the floor. The mother asked again, "If you are R's Auntie, tell me positively by knocking four times." Four distinct knocks were heard. Then there followed claw scratching on the mattress which beat out a rhythm as of marching soldiers.

The similarity of this diary and our interviews provides truth that the sound of scratching and a military style presence is valid when it comes to possession. Possession, Exorcism and Legion are all military terms referencing, the war between good and evil. Our interviews were conducted in 2009, where the Exorcist diary was written in 1949. Both describe the victims hearing the same scratching and marching sounds. Could this be the soul's early warning to prepare us for battle against our inner

Angel Or Devil

demons, or could it be the sound of the Devil himself? One thing for sure is ***"Something wicked this way comes."***

"And it shall be, when thou hearest the sound of marching, then thou shalt go out to battle." American Standard Bible Version (1901)

Introduction 2 from

THE STRANGE CASE OF THE POSSESSED

from *PARANOIA The Strange Case Of Ghosts, Demons and Aliens.* courtesy of Spooked Productions written by Christopher Saint Booth

www.paranoiabook.com

WATCH THE MOVIE
THE POSSESSED

a BOOTH BROTHERS documentary

www.thepossessedmovie.com

Exorcist Diary excerpts from *THE EXORCIST DIARY*
courtesy of Spooked Productions written by Christopher Saint Booth
www.theexorcistdiary.com
THE EXORCIST FILE a BOOTH BROTHERS documentary
www.theexorcistfile.com

Angel Or Devil

Angel Or Devil

BEGONE SATAN

Written in German by

REV. CARL VOGL

translated by

REV. CELESTINE KAPSNER, O.S.B.

A Sensational Expulsion of the Devil which occurred in Iowa in 1928.

S. B. St John's Abbey Collegeville, Minn.

Angel Or Devil

Nineteen hundred years ago, Christ, the Son of God, came upon this earth. He gained the victory over Satan, the Prince of this World, and founded His own Kingdom, the Church. He vested His Church with the same powers that He had received from the Father. *"As the Father sent Me, so I send you."*

When preparing her candidates for the ministry, Holy Mother Church hands these powers over to them that they may continue the mission of Christ's Kingdom on earth. Preparatory to Holy Priesthood the candidate receives the so-called minor and major orders. Among the minor orders is one called the Order of Exorcist. When the Bishop confers this order he pronounces the following significant words: You receive the power to place your hand upon those possessed and through the imposition of your hands, the grace of the Holy Ghost and the words of exorcism you shall drive evil spirits out of the bodies of those so possessed.

The Solemn and powerful meaning attached to this ceremony, not conferred in any of the other orders, can be gleaned from the words: Receive and impress upon your mind that you receive the right to place your hand upon those possessed.

Later on the Bishop invites the faithful to join him in asking that he who is to receive this order may be an effective agent in expelling the evil spirit from those possessed. He continues to pray that the candidate may become an approved physician of the Church through the gift of healing conferred upon her by the Almighty Himself.

The Church bases her action on the example of Christ Himself, Who frequently drove out evil spirits and endowed His disciples with full authority to do likewise. The superficial faith of our age regards such an order as superfluous. The reality of hell, devils, and cases of possession have been denied as myths of the dark ages. Even if Christ and the Apostles repeatedly emphasized the powers of the evil spirit, these are looked upon as purely superstitious. That Satan has succeeded in making man so indifferent regarding his actions of misleading men is one of his greatest and most advantageous accomplishments. People rarely listen to anything of a supernatural nature. Actual happenings of the I supernatural order in our times are all the more striking therefore and cannot so readily be dismissed by a mere shrug of the shoulders -- facts such as the numerous and indisputable miracles at Lourdes, the extraordinary visions, stigmata, abstention from food, and gift of languages of Theresa Neumann, the life of the Cure of Ars who was recently proclaimed a saint of the church, to whom for 35 years the sight of hell was constantly and really an ordinary experience. No less worthy of note are the facts in the cases of possession occurring in our times: the case of a possessed boy in Wemding, Suabia, Bavaria, 1891; the case in St. Michael's

Mission in Africa in 1906 of two girls possessed; the noted case of the Chinese woman Lautien in Honan, China, in 1926 and 1929, which was under the direction of Father Peter Heier, S.V.D., of Hague, N. D., now a Missioner in China, and several cases in Rockford, Ill since 1940.

The priest has frequent opportunities for using his power of exorcism. The blessings of holy water, its various uses in the blessing of houses and in the many other blessings and benedictions of the church in her sacramentals, are dependent upon this power. Pope Leo XIII in our own time composed a powerful and solemn prayer of exorcism for priests against the fallen angels and evil spirits. It is said that this Pope, after God permitted him to see in a vision the great devastation Satan is carrying on in our times, composed the prayer of exorcism in honor of St. Michael that is now recited in the vernacular as one of the prayers after Mass.

RECENT CASE OF POSSESSION & EXPULSION IN EARLING, IOWA

The following soul-stirring case of actual possession and successful expulsion, through the powers given to the Church over the evil one, is all the more striking in view of the above explanations. The facts herein narrated were testified to by the late Rev. Joseph Steiger, who was a personal witness of the scenes herein narrated. While conducting a mission in the parish of Earling in 1928, Father Theophilus Riesinger, O.M.Cap., asked the Rev. Pastor for permission to have a certain person, whom he believed possessed by the devil, brought into his parish, and to use the solemn formula of exorcism over her while she would be detained in the convent of the Franciscan Sisters who were active in the parish. Father Steiger happened to be a personal friend of Father Theophilus for many years past.

"What, another case of possession?" replied the pastor. "Are these cases still on the increase? You have already dispossessed the devil in a number of such cases!"

"That is indeed true. However, the Bishop has again entrusted this case into my hands. The lady in question lives at some distance from Earling. I should like to have her brought here, since it would create too much excitement in her home and perhaps would be the cause of many disturbances to the person herself."

"But why just here in my own parish?"

"It is just here in an outlying country district that the case may be disposed of in a quiet manner. Two places are available, either the Sisters' convent or in the sacristy here. So it is quite possible to relieve the unfortunate person of her burden without anybody out in the world becoming aware of it."

"My dear Father, do you really think that the Mother

Superior would permit anything like that to take place under her convent roof? I don't believe it. And it would be altogether out of the question to bring the person into my own house."

"My dear friend," smilingly replied the Father, "tell me this one thing. Will you give me your approval, should the Mother Superior be willing?

"Well, all right, but only under this condition. I do not believe that you will have any success at the convent."

"Thanks for your permission. The case is therefore settled, as the Mother Superior did give her consent from the very beginning. I have already made all arrangements with her for this case, provided you give your full approval."

Thus it was agreed to have the exorcism performed at the convent. The place was situated in the country, and as it was summer time, the people were actively occupied with their work in the open fields. No one would be any the wiser. Much less would anyone bother himself about what was going on. As a matter of precaution the case was again submitted to the Bishop, who called the pastor to himself to acquaint him with what he might expect to happen.

"So, my Father, you have given your consent to allow this to take place in your parish. Have you thought the matter over sufficiently?"

"Your Lordship, to be honest, I must confess that I was not very anxious to have it. I have a rather strong aversion for such unusual affairs. But Father Theophilus explained that my country parish together with the easy access to the convent would be just suitable for such an undertaking, and so I disliked to refuse."

"As Bishop I will caution you most emphatically that there may be some very serious consequences resulting to you in person. Should the Reverend Father not have enlightened you regarding the matter, then I wish to give you information based upon sound facts and similar experiences. The devil will certainly try his utmost to seek revenge on you, should you be willing that this unfortunate woman be relieved of this terrible oppression."

"Well, I hardly think that it will be as bad as all that. God's protecting hand will not fail me. The devil has no more influence than God permits. And if God will not permit it, the devil will not be able to harm me in the least. So I have no misgivings. I shall keep my word. I have given my consent, and for that very reason I would not care to withdraw it again. And should it entail some sacrifices, I shall be only too glad to bear them, if only an immortal soul shall benefit by it and be freed from the terrible stranglehold of that infernal being.

THE LADY IN QUESTION

The unfortunate woman was unknown to the pastor. She

lived far from Earling, and up to then he had heard nothing about her. The Capuchin Father had explained to him what her actual condition was, that she was a very pious and respectable person. Throughout her youth she led a religious, fervent and blameless life. In fact she approached the sacraments frequently. After her fourteenth year some unusual experiences manifested themselves. She wanted to pray, wanted to go to church and as usual receive Holy Communion. But some interior hidden power was interfering with her plans. The situation became worse instead of improving. Words cannot express what she had to suffer. She was actually barred from the consolations of the Church, torn away from them by force. She could not help herself in any way and seemed to be in the clutches of some mysterious power. She was conscious of some sinister inner voices that kept on suggesting most disagreeable things to her. These voices tried their utmost to arouse thoughts of the most shameful type within her, and tried to induce her to do things unmentionable and even to bring her to despair. The poor creature was helpless and secretly was of the opinion that she would become insane. There were times when she felt impelled to shatter her holy water font, when she could have attacked her spiritual adviser and could have suffocated him. Yes, there were suggestions urging her to tear down the very house of God.

Angel Or Devil

"Hallucination, a pure hysterical case, nervous spells."
Such easy explanation one will hear to account for the experiences. True, similar happenings do occur in nervous and hysterical cases. However, many doctors had this case in charge for years, and the woman was finally examined by the best specialists in the profession. But their thorough examinations resulted in the unanimous conclusion that the woman in question did not betray the least sign of nervousness, that she was normal in the fullest sense. There was not the slightest indication suggesting physical illness. Her undeniable and unusual experiences could not be accounted for. As the doctors could not help her, it was thought to see results in another field.

Many years passed. Finally, recourse was had to the Church and the supernatural powers of the priesthood. But a reserved and skeptical attitude was maintained for some years towards proceeding with exorcism. Examinations and observations were constantly made. It gradually became evident that strange preternatural powers were at play. The woman understood languages which she had never heard nor read. When the priest spoke the language of the Church and blessed her in the Latin tongue, she sensed and understood it at once, and at the same time foamed at the mouth and became enraged about it. When he continued in classical Latin, she regained her former ease. She was conscious at once when some one gave her articles sprinkled with holy water or presented her with things secretly blessed, whereas ordinary secular objects would leave her perfectly indifferent.

In short, when after years of trial and observation she had reached her fortieth year, the ecclesiastical authorities were finally convinced that here was a clear case of demoniacal possession. The Church must step in and deliver the poor creature from the powers of the evil one. The cause of the possession could not be ascertained. The woman herself could not give any information about this matter. Only later during the process of solemn exorcism was the cause made known.

Father Theophilus had spent many years giving missions in the United States and was familiar with cases of possession. Since he had already dispossessed the evil one in many instances, the Bishop entrusted this case to him. His stainless career, as well as his successful encounter in numerous possessions, singled him out as the one best suited to take hold of this case. He had little suspicion that he would meet with the severest experience as yet encountered by him and that matters of such a nature would confront him as would tax to the limit his physical endurance. Though this Capuchin Father is the very picture of health in his sixtieth year, yet he needed all available resources in order to carry the affair to a successful finish.

Angel Or Devil

The day agreed upon and approved by the Bishop for the exorcism at Earling, Iowa, was at hand. Besides the pastor and his sister, who was his housekeeper, and the Venerable Sisters, not a soul was aware of what was being undertaken. This secrecy had been strictly agreed upon beforehand. The main purpose of such procedure was chiefly to protect the name of the woman, lest anything of the affair might get out among the people and they might point to her and say: "This is the one who was once possessed by the devil." As she was to travel by train, it was found necessary to inform the personnel of the train. For should anything happen on the way, their help would have to be available in case the demoniacal influence should create any disturbance. This caution was not in vain, for the men had their hands full. They, however, did not know what the nature of the disturbance really was. The poor creature herself was only too willing to submit to the ecclesiastical procedure, so that she might be delivered from these terrible molestations. Yet she did not always have the necessary control over herself. She made this known after her delivery. Thus, the very night on which she arrived at the Earling station, she was so enraged over those who were there to meet her that she felt like taking hold of them and choking them.

Previous arrangements had been made for Father Theophilus to arrive that same night but by another route. The pastor took his own auto and went to meet him at the depot. Though the new car was always running in tip-top order it lacked the usual speed on this trip. Everything possible was tried, yet the car would not make any headway towards the station though no flaw could be found with it. The distance was not even worth mentioning, yet it took two hours for the pastor to arrive at the depot. He excused himself to his guest for causing such a delay and disappointment.

To which the latter replied very calmly: "My dear friend, I was not wrought up about it at all. I would have been much more surprised if everything had gone smoothly. Difficulties will arise; they must be expected to arise. The devil will try his utmost to foil our plans. While waiting I prayed constantly that the evil spirit would not be able to harm you, as I suspected that he would try to interfere with your coming, yea, that he would try to injure you personally." Now the pastor understood why his auto had balked. This was to be the first of many other unpleasant happenings. After such forebodings the reader can imagine that the missionary entered the car with some misgivings. But he took his precautions. He first blessed the auto with the sign of the Cross and then seated himself in the rear of the car. During the short ride to the rectory he quietly recited the rosary by himself lest something happen on the way to foil the attempt at exorcism.

Angel Or Devil

The two priests arrived without the slightest trouble Thank God, the woman also had arrived safely at the Sisters' convent. With this reassurance the difficult task could begin quietly on the morrow. However, that very night the enemy displayed his true colors. News was soon dispatched from the convent to the rectory next door that the woman caused difficulties from the very start. The well-meaning Sister in the kitchen had sprinkled holy water over the food on the tray before she carried the supper to the woman. The devil, however, would not be tricked. The possessed woman was aware at once of the presence of the blessed food and became terribly enraged about it. She purred like a cat, and it was absolutely impossible to make her eat. The blessed food was taken back to the kitchen to be exchanged for unblessed food; otherwise the soup bowls and the plates might have been crashed through the window. It was not possible to trick her with any blessed or consecrated article; the very presence of it would bring about such intense sufferings in her as though her very body were encased in glowing coal.

THE DECISIVE MOMENT HAD ARRIVE

All was quiet. Both the pastor and missionary, having offered up Holy Mass in the parish church that morning, went over to the convent where everything in a large room was in readiness for the exorcism. Fortified with the Church's spiritual weapons, they would dislodge Satan from his stronghold in the person of the possessed woman. How long would this process last? It was not to be expected that the devil would leave his victim without a fight. Certainly a few days would pass by before the powers of darkness would give in to the powers of Light, before the devils would let loose the soul redeemed by Christ, and return back to hell. It was well that neither the pastor nor the missionary knew with what kind of horde of evil spirits they would have to do battle.

The woman was placed firmly upon the mattress of an iron bed. Upon the advice of Father Theophilus, her arm-sleeves and her dress were tightly bound so as to prevent any devilish tricks. The strongest nuns were selected to assist her in case anything might happen. There was a suspicion that the devil might attempt attacking the exorcist during the ceremony. Should anything unusual happen, the nuns were to hold the woman quiet upon her bed. Soon after the prescribed prayers of the Church were begun, the woman sank into unconsciousness and remained in that state throughout the period of exorcism. Her eyes were closed up so tightly that no force could open them.

Father Theophilus had hardly begun the formula of exorcism in the name of the Blessed Trinity, in the name of the Father, the Son, and the Holy Ghost, in the name of the Crucified Savior, when a hair-raising scene occurred. With lightning speed the possessed dislodged herself from her bed and from the hands of her guards; and her body, carried through the air, landed high above the door of the room and clung to the wall with a tenacious grip. All present were struck with a trembling fear. Father Theophilus alone kept his peace.

"Pull her down. She must be brought back to her place upon the bed!"

Real force had to be applied to her feet to bring her down from her high position on the wall. The mystery was that she could cling to the wall at all! It was through the powers of the evil spirit, who had taken possession of her body.

Again she was resting upon the mattress. To avoid another such feat, precautions were taken and she was held down tightly by stronger hands.

The exorcism was resumed. The prayers of the Church were continued. Suddenly a loud shrill voice rent the air. The noise in the room sounded as though it were far off, somewhere in a desert. Satan howled as though he had been struck over the head with a club. Like a pack of wild beasts suddenly let loose, the terrifying noises sounded aloud as they came out of the mouth of the possessed woman. Those present were struck with a terrible fear that penetrated the very marrow of their bones.

"Silence, Satan. Keep quiet, you infamous reprobate! "

But he continued to yell and howl as one clubbed and tortured, so that despite the closed windows the noises reverberated throughout the neighborhood.

Awe-struck people came running from here and there: "What is the matter? What is up? Is there someone in the convent being murdered?" Not even a pig stabbed with a butcher knife yells with such shrieking howls as these.

The news travelled through the entire parish like a prairie fire: "At the convent they are trying to drive out the devil from one possessed." Larger and smaller groups were filled with terror as they approached the scene of action and heard with their own ears the unearthly noises and howlings of the evil spirits. The weaker members of the crowd were unable to endure the continued rage coming from the underworld. It was even more tense for those actually present at the scene, who with their own eyes and ears were witnesses to what was going on before them. The physical condition of the possessed presented such a gruesome sight, because of the distorted members of her body, that it was unbearable. The Sisters, even the pastor, could not endure it long. Occasionally they had to leave the room to recuperate in the fresh air, to gain new strength for further attendance at the horrible ordeal. The most valiant and self-composed was Father Theophilus. He had been accustomed to Satan's howling displays and blusterings from experiences with him in previous exorcisms. God seems to have favored him with special gifts and qualities for facing such ordeals. On such occasions, with the permission of the Bishop, he carried a consecrated host in a pyx upon his breast in order to safeguard himself against injuries and direct attacks by the evil one. Several times it happened that he was twisted about, trembling like a fluttering leaf in a whirl-wind.

One may ask: Does Satan dare at all to remain in the presence of the All Holy? How can he endure it? Does he not run off like a whipped cur? All we need to remember is that Satan dared to approach our Lord fasting in the desert. He even dared to take the Savior upon a high pinnacle at Jerusalem; and again he carried Him up on a high mountain-top. If he showed himself so powerful then, he has not changed since. On the contrary, the devils living in the possessed displayed various abilities and reactions. Those that hailed from the realm of the fallen angels gave evidence of a greater reserve. They twisted about and howled mournfully in the presence of the Blessed Sacrament, acting like whipped curs who growl and snarl under the pain of the biting lash. Those who were once the active souls of men upon earth and were condemned to hell because of their sinful lives acted differently. They showed themselves bold and fearless, as if they wanted every moment to assail the consecrated Species only to discover that they were powerless. Frothing and spitting and vomiting forth unmentionable excrements from the mouth of the poor creature, they would try to ward off the influence of the exorcist. Apparently they were trying to befoul the consecrated Host in the pyx, but failed in their purpose. It was evidently not granted them to spit upon the All Holy directly. At times they would spout forth torrents of spittle and filth out of the entrails of the helpless woman in order to give vent to their bitter spleen and hatred toward the All Holy One. You say torrents? Actually those present had to live through some terrible experiences. It was heartrending to see all that came forth from the pitiable creature and often the ordeal was almost unbearable. Outpourings that would fill a pitcher, yes, even a pail, full of the most obnoxious stench were most unnatural. These came in quantities that were, humanly speaking, impossible to lodge in a normal being. At that the poor creature had eaten scarcely anything for weeks, so that there had been reason to fear she would not survive. At one time the emission was a bowl full of matter resembling vomited macaroni. At another time an even greater measure, having the appearance of sliced and chewed tobacco leaves, was emitted. From ten to twenty times a day this wretched creature was forced to vomit though she had taken at the most only a teaspoonful of water or milk by way of food.

ONE OR MORE DEVILS

During this exorcism it was necessary to find out definitely whether the exorcist had to deal with one or more devils. It was also important for the exorcist to insist upon getting control over the person and of dispossessing the devil. On various occasions there were different voices coming out of the woman which indicated that un-numbered spirits were here involved. There were voices that sounded bestial and most unnatural, uttering an inexpressible grief and hatred that no human could reproduce. Again voices were heard that were quite human, breathing an atmosphere of keen suffering and indicating bitter feeling of disappointment. As is common in such experiences, Satan can, through the solemn exorcism of the Church, be forced to speak and to give answer. And, finally he can also be forced to speak the truth even though he is the father of lies from the very beginning. Naturally, he will try to mislead and to sidetrack the exorcist. It is also common experience that Satan at first does his utmost to sidestep the questions with clever, witty evasions, direct lies, shrewd simulations.

When Satan was asked in the Name of Jesus, the crucified Savior, whether there were more spirits involved in the possession of the woman, he did not feign in the least, but boastfully admitted that there were a number of them present. As soon as the name of

Jesus was mentioned, he began through the woman to foam and howl like a wild raving animal.

This ugly bellowing and howling took place every day and at times it lasted for hours. At other times it sounded as though a horde of lions and hyenas were let loose, then again as the mewing of cats, the bellowing of cattle and the barking of dogs. A complete uproar of different animal noises would also resound. This was at first so taxing on the nerves of those present that the twelve nuns were forced to take turns at assisting in order to save themselves and to have the necessary strength to continue facing the siege.

The exorcist: "In the name of Jesus and His most Blessed Mother, Mary the Immaculate, who crushed the head of the serpent, tell me the truth. Who is the leader or prince among you? What is your name?"

Devil, barking like the hound of hell. "Beelzebub."

Exorcist: "You call yourself Beelzebub. Are you not Lucifer, the prince of the devils?"

Devil: "No, not the prince, the chieftain, but one of the leaders."

Exorcist: "You were therefore not a human being, but you are one of the fallen angels, who with selfish pride wanted to be like unto God?"

Devil with grinning teeth. "Yes, that is so. Ha, how we hate

Him!"

Exorcist: "Why do you call yourself Beelzebub if you are not the prince of the devils?"

Devil: "Enough, my name is Beelzebub."

Exorcist: "From the point of influence and dignity you must rank near Lucifer, or do you hail from the lower choir of angels?"

Devil: "I once belonged to the seraphic choir."

Exorcist: "What would you do, if God made it possible for you to atone for your injustice to Him?"

Demoniacal sneering: "Are you a competent theologian?"

Exorcist: "How long have you been torturing this poor woman?"

Devil: "Since her fourteenth year."

Exorcist: "How dared you enter into that innocent girl and torture her like that?"

Sneeringly: "Ha, did not her own father curse us into her?"

Exorcist: "But why did you, Beelzebub, alone take possession of her? Who gave you that permission?"

Devil: "Don't talk so foolishly. Don't I have to render obedience to Satan?"

Exorcist: "Then you are here at the direction and command of Lucifer?"

Devil: "Well, how could it be otherwise?"

Let it be noted, too, that Father Theophilus addressed the devil in English, German, and again in Latin. And the devil, Beelzebub, and all the other devils, replied correctly in the very same tongues in which they were addressed. Apparently they would have understood any language spoken today and would have answered in it. Sometimes it happened that Father Theophilus, while in an exhausted state of mind, would make slight mispronunciations in his Latin prayers and words of exorcism. At once Beelzebub would intrude and shriek out. "So and so is right! Dumbbell, you don't know anything!"

Once it happened that Father Theophilus did not catch the words the devil spoke in an articulate mumbling voice. So he asked the pastor: "What did he say?" Neither had the pastor understood the devil. Then the nuns were interrogated: "What did he say?" One answered: "So and so, I think."

Then the devil bellowed and yelped at them: "You, I did not say that. Stick to the truth!"

Father Theophilus indeed was anxious to know why the father had cursed his own daughter. But he only received a curt uncivil reply: "You can ask him. Leave me in peace for once."

Exorcist: "Is then the father of the woman also present as one of the devils? Since when?"

Devil: "What a foolish question. He has been with us ever

since he was damned." A terrible, sneering laughter followed, full of malicious joy.

Exorcist: "Then I solemnly command in the name of the Crucified Savior of Nazareth that you present the father of this woman and that he give me answer!" A deep rough voice announced itself, which had already been noticed alongside the voice of Beelzebub.

Exorcist: "Are you the unfortunate father who has cursed his own child?" With a defiant roar: "No."

"Who are you then?"

"I am Judas."

"What, Judas! Are you Judas Iscariot, the former Apostle?"

Thereupon followed a horrible, woefully prolonged: "Y-e-s, I am the one." This was howled in the deepest bass voice. It set the whole room a-quivering so that out of pure fright and horror the pastor and some of the nuns ran out. Then followed a disgusting exhibition of spitting and vomiting as if Judas were intending to spit at his Lord and Master with all his might, or as if he had in mind to unloose his inner waste and filth upon Him.

Finally Judas was asked:

"What business have you here?"

"To bring her to despair, so that she will commit suicide and hang herself! She must get the rope, she must go to hell!"

"Is it then a fact that everyone that commits suicide goes to hell?" "Rather not."

"Why not?"

"Ha, we devils are the ones that urge them to commit suicide, to hang themselves, just as I did myself."

"Do you not regret that you have committed such a despicable deed?"

A terrible curse followed: "Let me alone. Don't bother me with your fake god. It was my own fault."

Then he kept on raving in a terrible manner.

THE DEMON JACOB

When the prayer of exorcism was renewed, the demon Jacob made his appearance with a healthy manly voice. As in the case of Judas, one could detect at once that he had been a human being. "Which Jacob are you?" asked the exorcist.

"The father of the possessed girl."

Later developments disclosed the fact that he had led a frightfully coarse and brutal life, a passionately unchaste and debased life. He now admitted that he had repeatedly tried to force his own daughter to commit incest with him. But she had firmly resisted him. Therefore he had cursed her and wished inhumanly that the devils would enter into her and entice her to commit every possible sin against chastity, thereby ruining her, body and soul.

Angel Or Devil

He also admitted that he did not die suddenly but that he was permitted to receive the sacrament of Extreme Unction. But this was of no avail because he scoffed at and ridiculed the priest ministering the sacrament to him. Later in the exorcism he made the following explanation: Whatever sins he had committed in this life might still have been forgiven him before death, so that he could have been saved; but the crime of giving his own child to the devils was the thing that finally determined his eternal damnation. Even in hell he was still scheming how to torture and molest his child. Lucifer gladly permitted him to do this. And since he was in his own daughter, he was not, despite all the solemn prayers of the Church, in the least disposed to give her up or leave her.

"But you will obey! The power of Christ and the Blessed Trinity will force you back into the pit of hell where you belong!"

Then followed a load roar and protest: "No, no, only spare me that!"

As the prayers of exorcism were continued, Jacob's mistress, who was in hell with him, also had to face the ordeal and give answer. Her high pitched voice, almost a falsetto, had already been noticed among the many other voices. She now confessed that she was Mina.

Mina admitted that the cause of her damnation was her prolonged immoral life with Jacob while his wife was still living.

But a more specific cause for her eternal woes in hell was her unrepented acts of child murder.

Exorcist: "You committed murder while you were still alive? Whom did you kill?"

Mina, bitterly: "Little ones." Evidently she meant her own children.

Exorcist: "How many did you actually kill?"

Mina, most unwillingly, curtly: "Three--no, actually four!" Mina showed herself especially hateful. Her replies were filled with such bitter hatred and spite that they far surpassed all that had happened so far. Her demeanor towards the Blessed Sacrament is beyond description. She would spit and vomit in a most hideous manner so that both Father Theophilus and the pastor had to use handkerchiefs constantly to wipe off the spittle from habit and cassock. Because of her unworthy communions, it was clear that the Blessed Sacrament, the Bread of Eternal Life, which should have been the source of her eternal salvation, turned out to be unto her eternal damnation. For she tried to get at the Blessed Sacrament with a burning vengeance and hatred. Out of this group of devils, Mina and Judas were the worst offenders against the Blessed Sacrament.

The reader would undoubtedly be misled if he were of the opinion that these questions and answers followed in regular order.

Angel Or Devil

It must be remembered that these battles and encounters with the devils extended over a number of days. At times the answers were interrupted by hours and hours of howling and yelling which could be brought into submission only by prolonged prayer and persistent exorcism. Often no further answers could be forced from the devils in any other way. Countless brats of devils also interrupted the process of exorcism by their disagreeable and almost unbearable interferences. As a result of these disturbances, the woman's face became so distorted that no one could recognize her features. Then, too, her whole body became so horribly disfigured that the regular contour of her body vanished. Her pale, deathlike and emaciated head, often assuming the size of an inverted water pitcher, became as red as glowing embers. Her eyes protruded out of their sockets, her lips swelled up to proportions equalling the size of hands, and her thin emaciated body was bloated to such enormous size that the pastor and some of the Sisters drew back out of fright, thinking that the woman would be torn to pieces and burst asunder. At times her abdominal region and extremities became as hard as iron and stone. In such instances the weight of her body pressed into the iron bedstead so that the iron rods of the bed bent to the floor.

According to the prescribed formula of the Church, the solemn exorcism began with the recitation of the Litany of All

Saints. All those present knelt and answered the prayers. At first the evil spirits remained peaceful, but when the petition, "God the Father of heaven," "God the Son Redeemer of the World," "God the Holy Ghost," "Holy Trinity one God," were said, the regular turmoil and gnashing of teeth began. At the petition, "Holy Mary," "St. Michael," the devils subsided as if struck by a bolt of lightning. A murmuring and muffled groaning arose at the mention of the choir of Angels and the Holy Apostles. At the words: "From the persecution of the devil," the evil spirit jumped up as if a scourge had hit him. "From the spirit of uncleanness," how he moaned and yelped like a beaten cur!

ACUTE CAUSE OF THE DEVIL'S PAIN

As the exorcism progressed, one could see that the benediction of the Blessed Sacrament pained the devil most acutely. That was always something unbearable for him. How he spat and vomited! He twisted and raved at the blessing with the relic of the Cross. Whenever the priest approached him with the cross and the prescribed words, "Look at the wood of the cross ! Begone ye powers of hell! The lion of the tribe of Juda shall conquer," he acted terribly.

"Stop it, stop it, I cannot bear it, I cannot listen to it!" he seemed to say.

And when the exorcist approached him with the relic of the

Cross hidden under his cassock, Satan became a raving maniac.

"Begone, begone," he howled, "I cannot bear it. Oh, this is torture! It is unbearable!"

The intercession, "Mary, the Immaculate Conception," caused him fearful agony. When he was addressed, "I command you in the name of the Immaculate Conception, in the name of her who crushed the head of the serpent," he wilted and languished. Then he bloated up the woman's body, and suddenly relaxed as one stunned.

HOLY WATER

Holy Water was also something hateful to Satan. Whenever he was approached with holy water he screamed: "Away, away with it, away with that abominable dirt! Oh, that burns, that scorches!" On one occasion a piece of paper bearing the inscription of a fake Latin prayer was placed on the woman's head. Even the good nuns believed that the prayer was genuine. In reality, the prayer consisted of words taken out of a pagan classic. The nuns were very much surprised that Satan remained so quiet under the experiment. The exorcist, however, knew the cause of the devil's tranquility. Immediately afterwards, a second prepared paper was placed on the head of the woman, which had been blessed beforehand with the sign of the Cross and holy water without anybody noticing it. In an instant the piece of paper was torn into a thousand shreds.

LITTLE FLOWER OF JESUS

The pastor had kept a small relic of the Little Flower of the Child Jesus in his sacristy in a small pyx without the knowledge of Father Theophilus. For protection's sake, he placed this in a side-pocket of his cassock one day and entered the convent where the exorcism was taking place. Just as the pastor entered the room, the devil began to rave: "Away, away with that! Away with the relic of the Little Flower, away with that weathercock!"

"We have no relic of the Little Flower," the exorcist exclaimed.

"Certainly, he who just entered has one," said the devil, indicating the pastor. At the same time the pastor approached with the relic. How the devil began to spit and to resist!

At other times the Little Flower played a more important part. One could also notice what a terrific battle Satan had with St. Michael.

ST. MICHAEL

At the very mention of St. Michael Satan began to recoil. He was tortured by that part of the prayer which refers to the solemn petition addressed to St. Michael. He absolutely refused to listen to the statement that St. Michael, as leader of the faithful angels, cast Lucifer together with his legions into the very abyss of hell. It was astounding how much he dreaded the prayer in honor of St. Michael commonly recited at the end of the Mass. The prayer is as follows: "St. Michael the Archangel, defend us in battle. Be our safeguard against the wickedness and snares of the devil. Restrain him, O God, we humbly beseech Thee, and do Thou, O Prince of the heavenly host, by the power of God cast him into hell with the other evil spirits, who prowl about the world seeking the ruin of souls. Amen."

Would that we as Christians recited this prayer in honor of St. Michael with greater fervor and devotion.

A rather peculiar circumstance induced Pope Leo XIII to compose this powerful prayer. After celebrating Mass one day he was in conference with the Cardinals. Suddenly he sank to the floor. A doctor was summoned and several came at once. There was no sign of any pulse-beating, the very life seemed to have ebbed away from the already weakened and aged body. Suddenly he recovered and said: "What a horrible picture I was permitted to see!" He saw what was going to happen in the future, the misleading powers and the ravings of the devils against the Church in all countries. But St. Michael had appeared in the nick of time and cast Satan and his cohorts back into the abyss of hell. Such was the occasion that caused Pope Leo XIII to have this prayer recited over the entire world at the end of the Mass.

CRUCIFIX AND RELIC OF THE CROSS

As indicated before, Satan dreaded the sign of the Cross, a

crucifix, or a relic of the true Cross. On one occasion a crucifix not made of wood was handed to Father Theophilus. This time Satan broke out in a sneering and ridiculing laughter: "Ha, so you arrived with a pasteboard cross! Since when did 'He' die on a paper cross? If my knowledge doesn't fail me, He was nailed to a wooden cross."

The crucifix was examined more closely and was indeed found to be made not of wood but of paper mache. On another occasion Satan made fun of the manner in which Christ was nailed to the cross. "Were not the feet of Jesus nailed one on top of the other, and not aside of each other?" Catherine Emmerich gives the same information. She says that the left foot was nailed first with a shorter nail. Then a longer and stronger nail, at the sight of which our Savior is said to have shuddered, was driven first through the right foot and then through the left. Those standing nearby at the crucifixion saw very plainly how the nail penetrated both feet.

This does not mean that we are now sure how the feet of our Savior were placed upon the cross, even if Beelzebub's statement tends to confirm the description given by Catherine Emmerich. We do not give the father of lies credit for being a reliable witness in such matters as the crucifixion, even if there is no doubt that many devils were personal witnesses to the crucifixion of Christ. In like manner I would have no one believe that we know for certain that Judas is in hell, just because he claimed that he was one of the damned in the case of possession at Earling. Holy Mother Church has never yet given a decision regarding this matter even though the words of our Savior about Judas are thought-provoking: "It would have been better if that man had never been born."

As the days passed by, a rather odd change manifested itself in the disposition of the pastor who began to experience a rather strong antipathy against the whole procedure of driving out of the devil.

ANTIPATHY AGAINST THE WHOLE PROCEDURE

The pastor could no longer bear the presence of Father Theophilus who had been a dear friend of his all along, and whom he had known intimately for years. If he would only be out of the way, out of sight! He now wished that he had refused to allow this exorcism to be performed in his parish, and that he had sent him directly out of his house. He became so worked up about it that he finally informed the exorcist of his ill feeling toward him and the whole affair. Father Th. did not show the least surprise. The case was still in the developing stages and it was only natural to suppose that the devil would have recourse to some source of temptation and annoyance in order to foil all attempts at dislodging him from the one possessed.

Furthermore, the devil used every occasion to display hatred for the pastor. "You are the cause of the whole affair, you are the one who tortures us so painfully," he burst out. The exorcist commanded Satan on one occasion as follows: "Be quiet, you hellish serpent. Let the pastor in peace once for all. He is not harming you in the least. I am doing this with the powers of exorcism."

This riled the devil all the more. He said "It is the pastor! He is at fault. Had he not given you permission to use his church and convent, you wouldn't be able to do a thing. And even today you would be helpless against us, if he would retract his assent."

This is an interesting proof of how the devil feels about and recognizes authority. He made this evident to every superior, while he acted rather civilly towards the subordinates. For that reason he never attacked the nuns nor the pastor's cook. All that the pastor or the mother superior had to do was to appear on the scene and the disturbance and raving was on. The mother superior once received such a blow across the face that she was thrust into the corner of the room. Satan repeatedly threatened Father Steiger, the pastor:

"You will have to suffer for this."

"You can't harm me anyway. I am standing under the protection of Almighty God, and against His power you are absolutely helpless, you detestable hellhound."

"Just wait! I'll make you repent that. I'll incite the whole parish against you and I will calumniate you in such a way that you will no longer be able to defend yourself. Then you will have to pack up and leave in shame and regret."

"If that be the will of God, then God be praised! But you are powerless against Him, you vile serpent, you man-killer!"

"Just wait! I will fix both you and your Lord and Master."

"Ha, how dare you speak that away against the Almighty, you despicable worm crawling in the very dust of the earth!"

"No, I cannot harm God directly. But I can touch you and His Church." And he continued with scorn and sarcasm: "Is it not true? Do you not know the history of Mexico? We have prepared a nice mess for Him there."

"Who? You devils?"

"Who else did it?

The whole credit is ours for bringing that situation about. He will learn to know us better. Lucifer is on His tracks and will make the kettle hot and heavy for Him. Ha, ha, ha!" A week later the devil advanced a little closer with his plans of revenge upon the pastor.

"Just wait," he threatened, "until the end of the week! When Friday comes, then . . ."

The pastor did not take this threat to heart. He was getting sick of listening to the howlings and yelpings of the devil day after day. Yet the pastor did indeed have a narrow escape on a certain Friday.

THE EXPERIENCE OF LIFE

Friday morning after Mass the telephone rang in the parish house. It was a call from a farmer, whose mother was critically ill. Would the pastor kindly come and administer the last sacraments to the dying? He wanted to call for the pastor with his own car, but somehow it was out of order and he couldn't locate the trouble. He had been trying to start it for over an hour, but in vain. It simply would not start. So he asked the pastor to come with his own auto, or to hire a taxi at the farmer's expense.

Within a quarter of an hour the pastor was on his way to help the sick woman, carrying the Blessed Sacrament with him. After dispensing the last sacraments, Father Steiger was again on the road towards Earllng. The road was familiar to him, for he had gone that way hundreds of times, by night and by day, and he knew every bump and stone along the way. He drove very carefully not only because the auto was new, but also because he was mindful of the devil's threats to trick him whenever the opportunity was ripe.

He prayed to his Guardian Angel and to St. Joseph, his Patron Saint, for a safe journey home. Suddenly as he was driving along, a dark black cloud appeared before him. It came just as he was about to pass a bridge over a deep ravine. Great God, it seemed as if his eyes were blindfolded! The next moment there was a crash, a smash-up which dumbfounded him. He found himself in a mess of ruins. The auto had crashed into the railing of the bridge with an indescribable force although he had jerked the car into low gear. The auto, now a complete wreck, was hanging on the iron trellis threatening every moment to drop into the deep abyss below. The noise of the crash was so loud that a farmer ploughing a field some distance away heard the noise and became greatly alarmed. Full of anxiety he hastened to the scene of the accident, "Good God, it's the pastor's car! Father, Father, what has happened? Are you hurt?" The pastor, scared to death, slowly crawled out from underneath the debris. Even the steering wheel was crushed to pieces. His legs would hardly hold him up. The wonder of it was that the rod of the steering wheel had not pierced his breast as frequently happens in such accidents. The farmer hastened home at once and soon reappeared with his own car. Leaving the wrecked car behind, he took the pastor, still shaking and in a deathlike pallor, into his own car and hurried directly to the nearest doctor to ascertain if there were any internal injuries. No, he was not seriously injured. The doctor discovered some external scars and a state of nervous excitement, but there was no sign of any internal injury. Thank God for that!

    Leaving the doctor's office, they drove straight to the parish house at Earling. There was no one at home, for they had all gone over to the covent to witness the exorcism. So the pastor also went there. He had hardly entered the room when he was greeted with a roaring laughter full of vengeance and bitter spleen: "hahaha-hahaha!" as if the devil were about to burst into a fit of malicious joy at besting him. "Today he pulled in his proud neck and was outpointed! I certainly showed him up today. What about your new auto, that dandy car which was smashed to smithereens? It served you right!"

The others looked wonderingly at the pastor. He was still pale but nothing ailed him otherwise.

"Reverend Pastor, is the devil speaking the truth?" they asked.

"Yes, what he says is true. My auto is a complete wreck. But he was not able to harm me personally." A quick reply came from the devil: "Our aim was to get you, but somehow our plans were thwarted. It was your powerful Patron Saint who prevented us from harming you."

News of this accident soon spread abroad and the people in deep sympathy with their beloved pastor, collected enough money to buy him a new car, so that the devil would receive no satisfaction from his pranks. Again and again the devil gleefully reminded the pastor of this incident and warned him to "be ready for a whole lot more of fun."

The devil also betrayed himself by saying that he is often the cause of similar accidents in order to bring people to quicker ruin. In this way he can get his revenge and give vent to his anger because lawsuits frequently result as a consequence, which, in turn, are responsible for much hatred and misunderstanding among people. The reader may make his own conclusions and resolutions regarding this. It cannot be so readily denied that the enemy of mankind actually plays a great part in such accidents. Is he not a "man-killer from the very beginning?" Hence a timely warning to those who use the auto for evil purposes, who decorate it with all sorts of nonsense and who even display figures alluringly immoral. The Church has provided a special blessing under the protection of St. Christopher against evil and disastrous influences. Therefore, it is customary to put one of these blessed medals or medallions in cars for safety's sake. St. Paul calls attention to the fact that the very air is filled with evil spirits.

SATAN'S SPEECHES

It should be noted that Satan did not use the tongue of the poor possessed woman to make himself understood. The helpless creature had been unconscious during the greater part of the trial. Her mouth was closed tight. Even when it was open there was not the slightest movement of the lips, nor were there any changes in the position of the mouth. The evil spirits simply spoke in an audible manner from somewhere within her. Possibly they used some inner organ of the body.

We know from the early Christian writers of the Roman period that the heathens frequently heard voices coming out of the idols. Catherine Emmerich also states that the evil spirits took up their abode in these idols and could clearly be heard to speak from within them in order to confirm the heathens in their delusion of idolatry. So it is conceivable how even some of the highly educated heathens worshipped these statues made by the hands of man, and why they offered sacrifices to them as if they were gods. They rendered to these idols the honor that belongs to God alone.

SATAN'S KNOWLEDGE CAN BE EMBASSING

The knowledge Satan had about the sins and the condition of the souls of those present was rather embarrassing to them. But in this case there were no disturbing revelations made along that line as there were only nuns and priests present. But even here he made insinuating remarks: "Is it not true that you did so and so in your past life, in your childhood days?" He made reference here to acts which were hardly remembered. The evil spirit, however, would not be quiet and tried to make a scene of things. So the answer was given. "If before God I am not guilty of greater faults in my later years than the sins of my childhood days, then I am not afraid."

Thereupon followed a most astonishing confession from the devil:"What you have already confessed, I do not know."

What follows from this? Apparently Satan knows only the sins that have not been confessed or repented. What has been submitted to the keys of the confessional seems to be out of his reach. It would seem that the sacrament of penance blots out or obliterates sins from the soul so as not to leave the slightest possibility for Satan to discover them. Through the sacrament of penance everything is, so to say, drowned in the abyss of God's mercy.

The rubrics in the Roman Ritual for exorcism, so wisely and so well established, demand that not only the exorcist, but also all witnesses and all those called upon to aid in subduing the possessed person, should make a thorough general confession, or at least a sincere act of perfect contrition before the process of exorcism begins. Once cleansed from sin they are more at ease in facing Satan and will not be subject to annoying remarks on the part of Satan for the sins committed in the past.

It happened about forty years ago, in a case of possession at Wemding, Germany, that during the process of exorcism the mistake was made of calling in the strongest men of the parish, men of good repute, to subdue a raving young boy. These good men did not realize with whom they had to deal. The horrible beast like howling and yelping was far less disconcerting than the hair-raising reproofs of the devil for the secret sins and other mistakes of one or the other of these men. He described them in minutest detail. Under such circumstances it is not surprising that few people care to be present at such exorcism, even if they could make themselves useful in many ways. Furthermore, it must be remembered that Satan, the father of lies, often twists small acts into unusually and seemingly grievous ones, making mountains out of molehills, so to speak, and at times purposely distorting them, mixing up truth with falsehood with the intention of creating the greatest disorder and most lasting enmity.

In order to avoid such inconvenient consequences, Father Theophilus, richer by mature experiences, undertakes his exorcism in consecrated or religious houses with only the assistance of priests and nuns. Even then things have happened. Satan shrewdly and sagaciously disclosed hidden things which made certain persons blush for shame; yes, he made them quiver with fear by threatening to expose them still more. All the more fortunate, then, that such experience that will henceforth take place under the seal of secrecy will not be broadcast to the whole world. Thank God for that!

Angel Or Devil

The meanness of the devil and the many odd happenings at Earling became common knowledge among the people in the bordering communities. The pastor of Earling, Father Steiger, had asked his people to unite in prayer and penance, and to make visits to the Blessed Sacrament so that the evil spirit might soon be mastered. Despite common knowledge of the unusual proceedings going on at the convent, not a single person asked out of curiosity to be permitted to witness the scene. Even if any one had asked, permission would not have been granted, except to priests from the neighborhood.

It has been intimated above that out of the voices coming from the possessed woman, four different ones could be very clearly distinguished. They announced themselves as Beelzebub, Judas Iscariot, Jacob, the father of the possessed woman, and Mina, Jacob's concubine.

The possessed woman had a clear memory of when her godless father cursed her and handed her over to the devil. She did not mention any further details about her unfortunate father, but it was learned from other sources that he was one of the worst persecutors of priests and of the Church. In sensual lust and excesses he was a monster of the worst type. He kept his distance from the Church and her sacramental ministration, and used every opportunity to ridicule spiritual things. Occasionally, he attended divine services on solemn feast days, but only to acquire new material from the sermons of the solemn functions to feed his ridicule and so bolster up his criticisms among friends and companions. Hence we can understand how he persisted in ridiculing the priest and his actions! when, even in his last moments, a merciful God granted him the grace of receiving the last sacrament of Extreme Unction. As you live, so you die. And his concubine, Mina, was fully his equal in this respect. Birds of a feather flock together. What was most surprising I was that such a wicked I and blasphemous father was blessed with such a virtuous child. Her sincere piety, her pure and innocent disposition, her diligent application, all were very apparent. Even during the period of possession the devil could not disturb her inner basic disposition because the devil has no power over the free will of a human being.

It was evident that, in addition to the above mentioned devils, there were also a great number of other unclean spirits in her. Among these the so-called dumb devils and avenging spirits made themselves especially prominent.

DUMB DEVILS AND AVENGING SPIRITS

The number of silent devils was countless. Apparently they were from the lower classes, for they displayed no marks of strength or power. Their voices were rather a confusion of sounds from which no definite answers could be distinguished. There was no articulate speech, rather a pitiful moaning and subdued howling. They could put up little resistance against the powerful effects of exorcism. It seemed as though they came and left in hordes, one crowd being relieved by others of the same type. They reminded one of a traveller who is suddenly overtaken by a swarm of mosquitoes. A few puffs of tobacco drive them away, but in short order they return and pester him again.

AVENGING SPIRITS

The avenging spirits were wild and violent, of rough and ill- mannered character. They were filled with hatred and anger against all human beings. Their very presence suggested an ugly and disgusting attitude --a mixture of hatred and envy, meanness and revenge, deception and trickery. These were precisely the ones that threatened to make the pastor rue his consent to this exorcism. They had in mind to stir up the whole parish against him by their misrepresentations, so that he would have to pack up and leave in disgust. One might presume from this that the devils are much to blame for bringing about misunderstandings between the pastor and the people. Not infrequently pastors tell of how they sacrificed themselves, even ruined their health, for the good of the people, but despite all their untiring efforts, some of the most inconceivable misinterpretations and misrepresentations had taken place in their parishes. Some people seem to find it their business to make the life of their shepherd so miserable that he is brought almost to the point of despair. All his good intentions bring him nothing but persecution of the worst sort. Hence it would not be amiss for pastors to use the small formula of exorcism periodically in order to protect their flocks from such meddling of the devil, or to use the prayers composed by Pope Leo XIII for just such an emergency.

The scheming and plotting of these avenging spirits almost succeeded in inciting the pastor of Earling to white heat against Father Th., his friend of long standing, doubtless with the intention of preventing the success of the exorcism. He was so wrought up over the procedure at times that he thought of bringing the whole affair to an abrupt close by driving Father Theophilus from his church and convent with the sharpest words of reproof.

NIGHT PROWLERS

During the process of exorcism, the evil spirits repeatedly made statements to the effect that they would tire and exhaust the pastor. One time in the middle of the night he was suddenly awakened by a disturbance in the room. Were rats gnawing somewhere? It seemed to be between the walls near his bed. Was there so much room there that the rats could run about so freely? During his fourteen years in this same house he had never experienced anything of the kind. Was he to be bothered with such miserable pests at last? He pounded the wall with his fist to scare away the rodents. But to no avail. He first used his cane, then his shoe, to pound on the wall. Instead of letting up, the noise became worse. Perhaps the night prowlers would disappear of their own accord. He waited and waited. They continued up and down between the walls, and even threatened to ruin them.

Father Steiger was in need of a good night's rest after all the disturbances during the day. An idea came that seemed altogether too foolish. Could there be some relation between these night prowlers and the evil spirits of the exorcism? Had not the devils threatened to tire him out? Perhaps this is what they meant after all. If so, then there is only one thing to do, and that is to use spiritual weapons against these intruders. Fortifying himself with his stole, the pastor again tried to sleep. At last the noise let up, but not altogether. "Wait, you cursed hell rats, I'll get rid of you yet!" Getting up again, he lit two candles before a crucifix and recited the small formula of exorcism against evil spirits. Aha! That was the language these hell rats understand. They took to flight and all was quiet. They seemed to have been spirited, blown off now, although all previous thumping and pounding on the walls had brought no results.

A few nights thereafter the pastor again spent a restless

night. Are the doors rattling? Is the house quaking? Oh, it's only a heavy express train going through the village, and these noises are only the after rumblings of the jarred earth. The railroad track was only a short distance away. He waited for the train to start from the depot, but he heard no move. Perhaps it's the rattling of machinery in the near-by electric shop!

Finally, the noise ceased. But suddenly it was heard again, this time right above the door. Maybe the door is ajar so that draft is swaying it back and forth. There was no door-stop to catch it, and so he had to get up again. But lo, the door was closed firmly. He took hold of the knob with a firm grip and pulled hard; it did not yield. What, is the devil again at his pranks to tire him out, to rob him of his night's rest? The pastor took the holy water, sprinkled, the door, windows, and room, and recited the short formula of exorcism. Again all was quiet. There was not a stir after that. "O you miserable Satan, now I know your stealthy cunning. Just wait, I'll soon teach you good manners."

It was learned later that other priests, who had attended the process of expelling the devil, experienced similar inconveniences and annoyances. Even worse things had happened to them. They would not retire after that without having holy water and the stole with them. The noises were often so persistent that one or the other of the priests was obligated to get up at night and seek the place and cause of the disturbances, and only after praying was he able to find peace again. Night prowlers of this kind have been met with in other cases of exorcism even long after the evil spirits had been driven out of the possessed person.

HOW THE POSSESSED WOMAN FARED

Every day the woman lost consciousness and became utterly helpless shortly after the formula of exorcism had begun. When the exercises ceased, she woke up and was herself again. She declared that she was unaware of what transpired during the exercises. Quite exhausted, she had to be carried to and from the place where the exorcism was performed. During all this time she could not eat solid foods, but nourishment in liquid form was injected into her. It was surprising to note how such a weak creature could vomit forth such quantities of material as indicated above. It was not unusual for her to vomit twenty to thirty times a day. The fact that, in her weakened condition, she could bear up under the daily strain of exorcism for three weeks seems incredible, especially when the terrible abuses upon her body inflicted by the devil, are taken into consideration. She suffered so intensely on one occasion that she assumed a death-like color, and seemed ready to pass away at any moment. "Great God, she is dying. I will hasten to get the holy oils!" broke out the pastor, who realized the terrible consequences for all concerned if she died under these conditions. The charge that the priest had caused her death through the strain of exorcism would certainly have been launched against them. Father Theophilus calmly replied on the basis of his long experience: "Just remain here, my friend; the woman will not die. Absolutely not. This manifestation is only one of Satan's cunning tricks. He cannot and will not be permitted to kill her. Absolutely not."

EXORCISM LASTED TWENTY-THREE DAY

The period of exorcism extended over an unusually long period of time. Never before did it take so long, as far as we know. It lasted just twenty-three days, however, in three different stages. And remember, the exorcism went on from early morning until late night. The devil tried his utmost to weaken the priests and nuns and to induce them to let up in their untiring efforts. The pastor could not always be present. His care of souls in the parish kept him away at times. Neither was he physically able to sacrifice so many hours of the night for this purpose. Thus it happened that many interesting and also terrible things took place in his absence to which, however, the others were trustworthy witnesses.

The solemn formula of exorcism was in progress for more than two weeks before there were any indications that the devil could be forced to depart from the poor helpless possessed woman. Even though Father Theophilus had succeeded in delivering her from a large number of devils through the great powers of the prayers and exorcisms, the four meanest and most persistent ones could not be dislodged for a long time. Satan seemed to have gathered up all the forces of hell to gain a final victory in this case.

HIGH COMMANDER

It was very evident that the forces of hell were under the direction of a high commander who, like a general and field marshal, sent forth new recruits for battle whenever the veterans, in their exhausted condition, were forced to retire. What pitiful sighs and pleadings they sent forth. One could hear voices to this effect: "Oh, what we have to put up with here; it is just terrible, all that we have suffered." There were other voices that kept on urging their fellow-devils not to let up: "And how we will again have to suffer and cringe under him, how he will torture us again if we return without having accomplished our task." They clearly referred to Lucifer as the torturer. In order not to give Satan and his hordes any peace whatever, Father Theophilus finally decided to continue the exorcisms himself throughout the night, expecting thereby to achieve his victory. He was blessed with a muscular body and with nerves of steel. He had tested these out by a rigorous and abstemious life of self-denial, which had given him great powers of endurance. And indeed it was something almost superhuman that was demanded of him. For three days and three nights he kept on without any intermission. Even the Sisters who alternated were on the verge of a breakdown. Yet the desired effect did not come It was only with the summoning of his last strength that the exorcist dared to continue. And at the close of the twenty-third day he was completely spent. He had the appearance of a walking corpse, a figure which at any moment might collapse. His own countenance seemed to have aged twenty years during those three weeks

ANTICHRIST

The reader may at this time be inclined to ask if the devil disclosed things that would be of general interest. For instance, the question of the Antichrist. What did Satan have to say about him?

It must be clearly borne in mind that the questions directed to the devil and the answers given by him were by no means an entertaining dialogue between the evil spirits and the exorcist. On occasions a long time intervened before an answer could be forced out of Satan. For the greater part, only a ghastly bellowing, groaning and howling was the result, whenever he was urged to answer under the powers of exorcism. It was often such a terrible drudgery, so exhaustingly tiresome and irritating, that on some days the exorcist was completely covered with perspiration. He had to make a complete change of attire as often as three to four times a day. Towards the end of those terrible days he became so weak, that he felt he could continue only with the special help of

Angel Or Devil

God. Yes, he even pleaded for the grace to be spared his own life. Curious questions not related to the present exorcism were never purposely asked. At times, however, it happened that some of the answers given by the devil himself suggested other questions not strictly pertinent to the case. On such occasions, Father Theophilus was snubbed by the devil with coarse and harsh replies: "Shut up, that is none of your business!" Satan often used the crisp Latin expression: *"Non ad rem!"* Which means, "not to the point," "that has nothing to do with this affair."

At one time Satan became rather talkative about the Antichrist. Remember the time he had so triumphantly referred to the Mexican situation, when he said that he would stir up a fine mess for Him (Jesus) and His Church, far more detrimental than hitherto. When asked whether he meant that the furious rage of the Antichrist would be directed against the Church of God, he asserted that that was self-evident and insolently continued: "Yes, Satan is already abroad, and the Antichrist is already born in Palestine. (On another occasion he also mentioned America.) But he is still young. He must first grow up incognito before his power can become known."

It is strange that Catherine Emmerich mentioned a similar period, when she gave a description of Christ's descent into hell after His death upon the cross. She related that "when the portals of hell were opened by the angels, there was a terrible uproar, cursing, scolding, howling and moaning. Individual angels were hurling hordes of evil spirits aside. All were commanded to adore Jesus. This caused them the greatest pain. In the center of it all there was a bottomless abyss as black as night. Lucifer was bound in chains and cast into this depth of darkness. All this happened in accordance with set laws. I heard that Lucifer, if I am not mistaken, would again be freed for a time about fifty or sixty years before the year 2000 A. D.

A number of other devils would be released somewhat earlier as a punishment and source of temptation to sinful human beings."

On one occasion, when Father Theophilus insisted that the devil should depart and return to hell, the devil replied in a growling tone: "How can you banish me to hell? I must be free to prepare the way for the Antichrist." And again he spoke out of the possessed woman: "We know a lot. We read the signs of the times. This is the last century. When people will write the year 2000 the end will be at hand."

Whether the "father of lies," as our Lord Himself styles Satan, spoke the truth, it is impossible to judge. At all events, we shall do well if according to our Lord's suggestion, we try to understand the signs of the times. That the powers of hell are putting up a desperate attempt to ruin the Church of Christ in our own times cannot be denied.

At one time the evil spirits howled and yelped fearfully when the prayers of exorcism were solemnly pronounced and when the blessings with the relic of the cross and the consecrated Host were given: "Oh, we cannot bear it any longer. We suffer intensely. Do stop it, do stop it! This is many times worse than hell!" These groans, indicating the attendant pain and suffering, cut to the quick.

"Therefore, depart at once, ye cursed! It is entirely within your power to free yourself from these sufferings. Let this poor woman in peace! I conjure you in the name of the Almighty God, in the name of the Crucified Jesus of Nazareth, in the name of His purest Mother, the Virgin Mary, in the name of the Archangel Michael!"

"Oh, yes," they groaned, "we are willing. But Lucifer does not let us."

"Tell the truth. Is Lucifer alone the cause of it?"

"No, he alone could not be. God's justice does not permit it as yet, because sufficient atonement has not yet been made for her."

This admission was valuable. It offered a greater inducement to arouse the members of the parish to increase their acts of expiation for the woman.

MORE ATONEMENT

In accordance with the request of their pastor, the parishioners gladly went to church to keep regular hours of adoration before the Blessed Sacrament. They prayed fervently for the destruction of the powers of Satan, and for the victory of the Church in delivering the victim from the tenacious grip of the devil. Following the directions of the ritual, the pastor kept on encouraging his people to private fasting and penance in order that their petitions would be more effective in strengthening the prayers of the exorcism. Our Lord Himself, when putting the devil to flight, and after beseeching all to pray, had told the Apostles that this kind of devils can only be driven away by prayers and fasting. The devil's own statement, that sufficient penance had not been done, helped to bring about more fervent prayers and more rigorous penances. The faithful flocked to church in large numbers from early morn until late in the evening in order that, by their prayers, they might add their mite to the work of the Church in this her mission. The exorcism could not continue much longer as the reserve strength of those actually assisting was being vitally sapped.

BATTLE BETWEEN GOOD AND EVIL SPIRITS

It was during this time that the poor woman admitted

during her periods of rest that she had visions of horrible battles between the good and evil spirits. Countless numbers of evil spirits continually arrived. Satan tried his utmost not to be outdone this time. The good angels came to assist at the exorcism. Many approached seated on white horses (Apocalypse 19, 15) and under the leadership of St. Michael, completely routed the infernal serpents and drove the demons back to the abyss of hell.

THE LTTLE CHILD OF JESUS

The Little Flower of Jesus also appeared to the woman during these crucial days and spoke these consoling words to her: "Do not lose courage! The pastor especially should not give up hope. The end is soon at hand." This occurred on a certain evening when, to their surprise, the nuns and the pastor's sister suddenly noticed a cluster of white roses on the ceiling. After a while the vision gradually disappeared. The pastor noticed the anxious gaze of these ladies directed towards the ceiling, but he himself did not see the flowers. The words of encouragement from the Little Flower gave a new impetus to the priests. Now they knew that victory was not far off. During the latter days the devils betrayed great fear lest they be forced to return to hell. Father Th. insisted upon their departure again and again. They pleaded pitifully: "Anything but that, anything but that." To be banished to another place, or into another creature would have been more bearable.

They did not want to "But you are already in hell."

"True, true," they groaned, "we drag hell along with us. Yet it is a relief to be permitted to roam about the earth until (at the last judgment) we shall be cast off and damned to hell for eternity."

THE DEVILS DEPART

Gradually the resistance of the devils began to wane. They seemed to become more docile. Their bold, bitter demeanor gave way to more moaning and despairing tones. They could not bear the tortures of exorcism any longer. With great uneasiness they explained that they would finally return to hell. But how often they are deceptive and unreliable! Experience teaches us that at times they pretend to leave the possessed entirely at ease for a while, in order to sidetrack the unwary observer and thus outwit him. For this reason Father Th., almost completely exhausted, demanded in the name of the Most Blessed Trinity that at their departure the devils should give a sign by giving their respective names.

"Yes," they promised emphatically.

It was on the twenty-third day of December, 1928, in the evening about nine o'clock that, with a sudden jerk of lightning speed the possessed woman broke from the grip of her protectors and stood erect before them. Only her heels were touching the bed. At first sight it appeared as if she were to be hurled up to the ceiling. *"Pull her down ! Pull her down" called the pastor while Father Th. blessed her with the relic of the Cross, saying: "Depart, ye fiends of hell! Begone, Satan, the Lion of Juda reigns!"*

At that very moment the stiffness of the woman's body gave way and she fell upon the bed. Then a piercing sound filled the room causing all to tremble vehemently. Voices saying, "Beelzebub, Judas, Jacob, Mina," could be heard. And this was repeated over and over until they faded far away into the distance.

"Beelzebub, —Judas, —Jacob, —Mina." To these words were added: "Hell—hell—hell!"

Everyone present was terrified by this gruesome scene. It was the long awaited sign indicating that Satan was forced to leave his victim at last and to return to hell with his associates.

What a happy sight it was that followed! The woman opened her eyes and mouth for the first time, something that had never taken place while the exorcism itself was going on. She displayed a kindly smile as if she wanted to say: "From what a terrible burden have I been freed at last!"

For the first time in twelve years she uttered the most holy name of Jesus with child-like piety: *"My Jesus, Mercy! Praised be Jesus Christ!"*

Tears of joy filled her eyes and those of all in attendance.

Amid the first rejoicings, the witnesses were not aware of

the terrible odor that filled the room. All the windows had to be opened. The stench was unearthly, simply unbearable. It was the last souvenir of the infernal devils who had to abandon their earthly victim.

What a day of joy it was for the whole parish! *Te Deum laudamus!* Holy God, we praise Thy name! Not unto us, not unto us, O Lord, but to Thy name be glory and praise!

From that time on the woman, always sincerely good, pious and religious, frequently visited the Blessed Sacrament and assisted at Holy Mass. She received Communion in a most edifying manner. That which was so terrible for her while she was under the torturing powers of Satan is now the peaceful joy, of her heart and soul.

THERESA NEUMANN

Theresa Neumann of Konnersreuth was also concerned in this affair. A Bishop of Switzerland, who had been well informed about the above case, paid a visit to Theresa Neumann. And since it was Friday, he asked her while she was in one of her ecstatic visions whether she was aware of the terrible case of demoniacal possession in America. She immediately answered:

"Is it not so? You mean the case in Earling, Iowa, at which some priests scoffed, and about which others were indifferent?"

Then followed an astounding announcement: "The good

woman will later be possessed. This will be for her own personal benefit, for her own purification and complete atonement."

Furthermore, the stigmatic woman of Konnersreuth had a terrible vision on the Feast of St. Michael, pertaining to the exorcism that had taken place in Earling. She witnessed the frightful battle between the angels of heaven under the leadership of St. Michael and the infernal demons under the command of Lucifer. She was so shocked and confused by it that she said:

"If it be not against the will of God, I will ask Him never again to permit me to witness anything so terrible."

It was by far the worst vision she had ever experienced.

Father Theophilus, basing his opinion on his numerous experiences with cases of possession, believes that the hour of the Antichrist is not far distant. Lucifer himself was present for about fourteen days in the Earling case. With all the forces of hell at his disposal he tried his utmost to make this a test case. Once Father Th. saw Lucifer standing visibly before him for half an hour--a fiery being in his characteristically demoniac reality. He had a crown on his head and carried a fiery sword in his hand. Beelzebub stood alongside of him. During this time the whole room was filled with flames. Lucifer was cursing and blaspheming in a terrible rage: *"If I could, I would have choked you long ago. If I only had my former powers, you would soon experience what I could do to you."*

Through the powers of Christ he had been deprived of his original might as even now through exorcism his influence was further diminished. Father Th. asked him one time: *"What can you accomplish, you helpless Lucifer?"*

To which he replied: *"What could you do, if you were bound as I am?"*

Father Th., who has had nineteen cases of possession under his care within recent years, seems convinced that present indications point to the beginning of a great battle between Christ and Antichrist. He also seems to have learned that Judas will appear as Antichrist in this manner, that a human person, soon after birth, will be controlled and completely ruled by him. Besides the Antichrist, there will be the false prophet, in reality Lucifer, who will perform wonderful deeds and false miracles. He will not be born of a woman, but will construct a body for himself out of earthly matter in order to plot as a man among men. But the faithful need not fear, for all the powers of heaven with its countless angels will be fighting on their side.

SUPPLEMENT

The above account gives only the exorcisms that took place at Earling, Iowa. She was possessed the first time in 1908 through her aunt, Mina, known among the people as a witch. The latter had placed a spell on some herbs which she placed among the woman's food. Father Theophilus freed her from this possession June 18, 1912. She became possessed again due to the curses hurled against her by her wicked father. The Earling exorcism was in three stages: *Aug. 18-26, 1928; Sept. 13-20, 1928; Dec. 15-22, 1928.* There were still later possessions but of a milder nature.

This woman was born in 1882, is of small stature and had but an elementary education. She preserved her virginity though she had been exposed to severe trials. She is still among the living, and recently through private revelations from Christ has been advocating the spread of perpetual adoration of Christ in the Blessed Sacrament as a remedy for a lasting peace.

The purpose of this pamphlet is not to frighten timid souls but rather to encourage those of strong faith to continue to give battle to the evil one. It is also a timely warning to sinners to amend their lives from sin to virtue. It is precisely through the cooperation of sinners that the devil has such power on earth. It also gives all of us the assurance that the prayers of the Church and the penance of the faithful in cooperation with her today have still the same effect over our enemies as did Christ's personal dealings with the evil spirits during His early sojourn.

Holy Mother Church has not made any official decision regarding the Earling case and hence the statements made in this pamphlet are only of a private nature and are to be accepted merely on their face.

TESTIMONY OF THERESA WEGERER, FATHER STEIGERS'S HOUSEKEEPER

"I was a witness to almost the whole period of the exorcism of the Earling possession case and I can truthfully say, that the facts mentioned in Begone Satan are correct. Some of the scenes were even more frightful than described in the booklet. There is not the slightest doubt in my mind, that the devils were present and I will never forget the horrible scenes, vile, filthy, and dirty, as long as I live. All the nuns asked for a change and were transferred the next year.

"The woman came back to Earling over a distance of a thousand miles four months after the exorcism to make a novena of Thanksgiving. This was at the bidding of Christ Himself. During her stay she boarded with the Schimorowsky family. She told me how our Blessed Lord appears to her frequently and encourages her to be faithful."

Dr. John Dundon
Physician and Surgeon
1228 E. Brady St., Milwaukee, Wis.

Angel Or Devil

Rev. Celestine Kapsner, O.S.B.
St. John's Abbey
Collegeville, Minn.

Dear Father Kapsner:

We wish to indorse your pamphlet "Vade Satana" as a potent aid to faith in the value of sacramentals, relics of the saints and prayer. No more vivid picture has been presented to us of the losing battle against the "camp of Christ." Nothing has made our insistent floundering from the "camp of Christ" to the "camp of the devil" appear so absurd. The memory it has instilled of the hatred of Satan and the eternal misery of his permanent army, evokes a continuous inventory of one's life, savoring of the minuteness of the final judgment. That it will save many souls we have no doubt. That some will borrow fruitless· fright is also possible, but for them one must say that if the picture is terrible the real thing must be worse, Agony is the lot of all at least once. Satan has seemed too unreal. It would be a pity if this pamphlet were to be suppressed because some weak souls have been made to sense him more vividly than the author intends.

We were granted an interview with the exorcist, Father Theophilus, after reading your account of the diabolical possession. We treasure the experience as an intimate glimpse into the life of a pious priest very gifted in a specialty which should command the patronage of the medical profession, rathe.r than to be allotted to the realm of superstition or necromancy. We anxiously await his complete report of the Earling

Yours very truly,

J. D. Dundon, M.D.

"Mary Crushes The Serpent" sequel 15c.
"Angels, Our God Given Companions and Servant" 15c.

THE END

IN RESPECT AND MEMORY
OF
ANNA ECKLUND
EMMA SCHMIDT

Angel Or Devil

WATCH THE MOVIE!

THE EXORCIST FILE - HAUNTED BOY

As seen in RedBox.(Top Rental 2014) Winner of Best Feature Film-Full Moon Horror Film Festival.

While filming a haunted asylum in St. Louis, Missouri, documentary filmmakers uncover a secret diary of the infamous 1949 exorcism involving a 13 year old child possessed by the devil that later inspired the book and movie "The Exorcist"

www.theexorcistfile.com

CREDITS & THANKS

THE CAST AND CREW OF

SPOOKED TV

Keith Age ~ Rosemary Ellen Guiley

Anita Tallbull ~ John Zaffis

Gregory Myers ~ Sandra Oates~

Juli Velazquez~ Dewi Morgaine

Marcus ~Joyce Wesbrooks

Troy Taylor ~ John Whitman

The Roff House~ The Vennum House

The Town Of Watseka

Angel Or Devil

SPECIAL THANKS
REV. CARL VOGL
REV. CELESTINE
E. W. STEVENS
GOD
Philip Adrian Booth
Rachel Marie Booth
Alyssa and Gabiel for
making me a better man

ABOUT THE AUTHOR

Christopher Saint Booth born in Yorkshire, England started his career at an early age. Influenced by The Beatles, singing and strumming at the age of four. Atlantic crossing brought them to Canada where at the age of thirteen he were writing and performing at the local establishments. In 1978 he was invited to combine forces with, Juno award winner, Sweeney Todd. (London Records) Worldwide touring commenced immediately as their new gold album paved his way to sunny California. Upon arriving in Los Angeles, greeted with a publishing deal (RCA Music) he began writing vocalizations and musical scores for film, cable and television.

Desires of new creative outlets began development, now reaching out to the visual side of entertainment. Audio with Video studios were soon built to quench this creative thirst. Christopher, a successful film and music Director, Producer, Production Designer and Composer has written, edited, animated, directed and scored some of Billboard's Top Ten releases including, Film Features, Erotic Thrillers, Music Videos and worldwide releases.

Internationally renowned for his provocative style,Independent films soon broadened the horizon. Financing a million-dollar HD digital domain in Los Angeles California, this is where he would design and build his ultimate dreams. As well as endorsed by an array of electronic arts manufacturers, no boundaries would be left untouched. For every new technical toy that the eyes and ears could ever dream of soon became vivid. As an Apple licensed developer and 3rd party designer for SoftImage, AMP, APDA and Microsoft, Booth continued to design the future of entertainment and media for all platforms. New concepts with slick designs go hand in hand with the latest web technology

Angel Or Devil

With over 100 features behind him built all from scratch with the insight of what's happening tomorrow for the people today. A panoramic view of freedom with the fresh scent of change inspires this Saint to create a brave new world for your eyes and ears. Christopher is married to Rachel Marie and the father to Gabriel & Alyss B.

Christopher is an Author, Producer and Director of films and documentaries for Syfy, Chiller, NBC Universal, Spooked TV Productions, At&t, Vimeo, Apple iTunes, Netflix, Roku and more worldwide. CEO of Spooked Television Releasing.

Films include Dead Still (Syfy), Death Tunnel (Sony Pictures), The Possessed, Spooked, Children Of The Grave (Syfy Channel/NBC Universal), The Exorcist File-Haunted Boy (Redbox), Children Of The Grave 2, Soul Catcher and DarkPlace. For sales more info; www.spookedtv.com

<u>Christopher Saint Booth</u>
Official Site: www.christophersaintbooth.com
FaceBook:www.facebook.com/christophersaintbooth
Twitter: www.witter.com/sainttweets

Angel Or Devil

OTHER BOOKS BY CHRISTOPHER SAINT BOOTH

PARANOIA THE STRANGE CASE OF GHOSTS, DEMONS AND ALIENS

Journey beyond the screams with filmmaker Christopher Saint Booth as seen on Syfy, Chiller and Sony Pictures. Uncover the real stories behind the history and haunting of the Booth Brothers scariest films, cases and locations including Death Tunnel, Spooked The Ghosts Of Waverly Hills Sanatorium, Children Of The Grave, The Possessed and The Exorcist File. In this human emotional search for the afterlife, explore supernatural evidence, theories and techniques from the leading paranormal investigators, sensitives and demonologists.

www.paranoia.book.com
ISBN-13: 978-0692488904

THE EXORCIST DIARY

What intrigued me about this diary was that "The Exorcist" was by far the scariest horror movies of all time based on true events. The actual case involved a boy not a girl as portrayed in the

Angel Or Devil

movie. We went to St. Louis to find out the truth and uncover the real diary and we did just that. Documented by 14 priests this diary chronicles the horrific story of "The Exorcist" and a boy possessed by the devil. For the first time read the unedited diary of the boy's possession and exorcism. Learn the facts and truth about one of the most darkest supernatural cases known to man.

www.theexorcistdiary.com

ISBN-13: 978-0692536698

Also available on Amazon, Barnes and Noble and at www.spookedtv.com

SPOOKED TV

Feature Films, Documentaries, Music and Books

www.spookedtv.com

VIDEO ON DEMAND

SPOOKEDtv-OD

www.spookedtv-od.com

Movies streaming on

AMAZON INSTANT VIDEO

(search Booth Brothers)

Angel Or Devil

www.amazon.com

ORIGINAL SOUNDTRACKS

Amazon and iTunes

www.itunes.apple.com/us/artist/christopher-saint/id211036282

www.cdbaby.com/Artist/ChristopherSaint1

PARANOIA AUDIO BOOK EXPERIENCE

https://itunes.apple.com/us/album/paranoia-audio-experience/id1079060031

http://www.cdbaby.com/cd/christophersaintbooth2

Publishing House

SPOOKED TV PUBLICATIONS

18017 CHATSWORTH STREET #130

GRANADA HILLS, CA 91344

Email:

info@spookedproductions.com

Phone: 310-498-9576

VISIT US ON FACEBOOK

www.facebook.com/SPOOKEDtv

www.facebook.com/christophersaintbooth

TWITTER

Angel Or Devil

www.twitter.com/spookedtv

OFFICIAL SITE
WWW.SPOOKEDTV.COM
ANGEL OR DEVIL
Spooked TV Publications
ISBN-13:978-0692663646
ISBN-10:0692663649
DEVIL OR ANGEL ©2106 SPOOKED PRODUCTIONS

INTRODUCTIONS
WRITTEN BY CHRISTOPHER SAINT BOOTH FROM
PARANOIA The Strange Case Of Ghosts, Demons and Aliens and THE EXORCIST DIARY

THE WATSEKA WONDER
"AMERICA'S FIRST DOCUMENTED POSSESSION" BY E. W. STEVENS
CHICAGO: REL1G10-PH1LOSOPHICAL PUBLISHING HOUSE. 1878.

BEGONE SATAN
WRITTEN BY REV. CARL VOGL
translated by REV. CELESTINE KAPSNER, O.S.B.
SPOOKED TV PUBLICATIONS 18017 CHATSWORTH STREET #130
GRANADA HILLS, CALIFORNIA, 91344 USA
Email: info@spookedproductions.com
SPOOKED TV PUBLICATIONS

Angel Or Devil

18017 CHATSWORTH STREET #130

GRANADA HILLS, CALIFORNIA, 91344 USA

Email: info@spookedproductions.com

ANGEL OR DEVIL

ISBN-13:978-0692663646

ISBN-10:0692663649

www.spookedtv.com

Photography and Art Design by Christopher Saint Booth

Models: Rachel Marie and Ava Aurora

Additional research Denise Mendenhall

Angel Or Devil Art ©2016 Christopher Saint Booth

The Possessed ©2009 Spooked Productions.

The Exorcist File ©2014 Spooked Productions

The Haunted Boy ©2010 Spooked Productions

THE EXORCIST DIARY©2015 Spooked Productions

PARANOIA The Strange Case Of Ghosts, Demons and Aliens ©2015 Spooked Productions

This book is distributed as a serious reference study in possession and is not attended in anyway to endorse or exploit any religion or the people portrayed in this book and these true journals. © Creative Commons

DEVIL OR ANGEL ©2106 SPOOKED PRODUCTIONS

All Rights Reserved. No part of this publication may be reproduced or transmitted in any form or by any means, electronic or mechanical, including photocopy, recording, or any information storage and retrieval system, without permission in writing from the publisher.

Angel Or Devil

www.angelordevilbook.com

www.ingramcontent.com/pod-product-compliance
Lightning Source LLC
Chambersburg PA
CBHW032042090426
42744CB00004B/97